Plants

of the

Cherokee

Medicinal, Edible, and Useful Plants of the Eastern Cherokee Indians

By William H. Banks, Jr.

© 2004 by Great Smoky Mountains Association

WRITTEN BY: William H. Banks, Jr.

EDITED BY: Steve Kemp
DESIGNED BY: Joey Heath
EDITORIAL ASSISTANCE BY: Ila Hatter, Janet Rock, and Eva Millwood

PRINTED ON 30% POST-CONSUMER WASTE RECYCLED PAPER

4   5   6   7   8   9   10   11   12   13   14   15   16   17   18

Great Smoky Mountains Association is a private, nonprofit organization which supports the educational, scientific, and historical programs of Great Smoky Mountains National Park. Our publications are an educational service intended to enhance the public's understanding and enjoyment of the national park. If you would like to know more about our publications, memberships, and projects, please contact: Great Smoky Mountains Association, P. O. Box 130, Gatlinburg, TN 37738, (888) 898-9102. www.SmokiesInformation.org

Contents

Plants of the Cherokee: Medicinal, Edible, and Useful Plants of the Eastern Cherokee Indians

Foreword

After languishing for 50 years in libraries, archives and attics around the southern Appalachian region, the following manuscript by William Banks was brought to the attention of Great Smoky Mountains Association by two of the organization's most active members: Jerry Coleman and Ila Hatter. Mr. Coleman and Ms. Hatter live near the Cherokee reservation in western North Carolina and are recognized experts on edible and medicinal plants in the area. They were overjoyed to discover the existence of the manuscript and devoted themselves to seeing that it be published.

Staff at the National Park Service and Association were equally excited to learn of Banks' masters thesis. During the early 1950s, when Banks did his research, there were still quite a few elder Cherokee and others who continued the old ways of using wild plants for a wide variety of medicines, food, crafts, and other purposes. Today, attempting to conduct such research would be much less fruitful.

It should be mentioned that Banks' thesis advisor and mentor, Dr. A. J. Sharp, was one of the most widely recognized and respected experts on the botany of the Great Smokies and southern Appalachians. His career as botanist, professor, writer, and advisor spanned more than 60 years. Sharp's role as overseer on this project lends it great credence.

A Note on Plant Names

In the years since this manuscript was written, many of the scientific names of plants have been changed to reflect a better understanding (largely through DNA research) of plants' relationships to each other. To make this book pertinent to contemporary users, we have used the modern versions of plant names. Consequently, the scientific (and common) names for plants used in this book should match those that appear in today's commonly used field guides to wildflowers, trees, and ferns.

Chapter 1

Introduction

In September 1951, a study of the ethnobotany of the Cherokee Indians was suggested to me as the subject for my Master of Science thesis at the University of Tennessee, by Dr. Aaron J. Sharp. I was immediately enthused about the idea for a number of reasons.

The research involved would necessarily deal with people as well as plants, thus combining my greatest interests. The project would also afford an excellent opportunity to work in close contact with a botanically rich area, thus enabling me to strengthen my knowledge of nature.

My work on the project did not actually begin until some seven months later. In the intervening period, however, preparatory work was undertaken. I enrolled in anthropology courses at the University of Tennessee. Therein were gleaned concepts, which helped in the gathering of factual data, suggested some of the dynamics of the culture under observation, rounded the discussions appearing in the appendix, and aided immeasurably my understanding of the Cherokee Indians.

In May 1952, steps were taken to provide for my wife and myself a place of residence for a three month field trip. With the help of Mr. Joe Jennings, reservation superintendent, and Mr. Sam Gillam, agricultural agent of the reservation, a room was located. The room was rented from the 73-year-old widow of a "full-blooded" Indian, her daughter, and her full-blooded son-in-law. Once established, it was a matter of discovering contacts, gaining their confidence and getting information from them pertaining to Cherokee usage of plants.

Work progressed slowly at first, chiefly through my inexperience in knowing where to start. The task of gathering information on the some 800 plants which James Mooney (Mooney, 1890) indicated to be the complete Cherokee repertoire was staggering for the short length of time allotted. I resolved to concentrate on a smaller number of plants, but to gather more complete information on these. At the same time, effort was made to gather data on as many plants as time and circumstances permitted.

After arriving in Cherokee, North Carolina in June 1952, my first step was to obtain information concerning likely informant "prospects" from Miss Mary Ulma, librarian of the Cherokee Government School. Miss Ulma was instrumental in the organization of a Medicinal Herb Contest which appeared in the Cherokee Indian Fair in October 1951. She supplied me with a carbon copy of the contest entries, listing the plants of each exhibit. She also furnished the 10 names of the contestants and information on how to locate their homes.

With this list of 10 names, I set out to contact persons and to obtain from them additional and more complete information.

Five of these persons proved helpful in giving information, one person had moved to New Jersey, two were considered to be unreliable and were not contacted, one lady was reticent to impart any information, and the last was a white person, not contacted. Through these persons and Mr. John Witthoft, I contacted five additional persons who were of great help. Mr. Witthoft graciously lent me his personal file listing plants with their Cherokee names and usages. These field notes were taken from at least three informants not included above. Two of these three persons are deceased.

The general pattern of approaching a likely informant was (1) introduction, (2) light conversation or remarks on a neutral subject—weather, crops, local events, etc., (3) statement of the writer's purpose, (4) the exchange of ideas.

Most informants were quite willing to tell what they knew. One person refused to help, and another, Yute Jumper, suddenly decided to stop giving information. On my third call to the Jumper cabin, I found the 83 year-old Indian "out" and on the fourth call was told that he, Jumper, no longer wanted to tell his secrets. A theory some of the older Indians retain is that medicines lose their potence if the knowledge of their use becomes common. This may well be, for as it will be seen, the efficacy of a medicine may depend on a psychological effect.

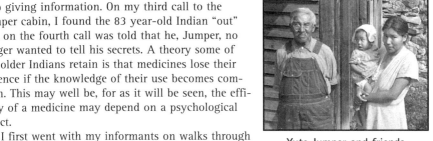

Yute Jumper and friends

I first went with my informants on walks through the shaded woods, stopping at crystal springs for refreshing drinks and calling occasionally at the cabin of a neighboring Indian. Along the way the guide would pick up a familiar plant, tell how it is, or was, used and move on. I collected these plants and identified them later either with a manual or by having them identified at the University of Tennessee.

This method, although the most satisfactory way to gather information on native plants, proved very slow. I could take such hikes with informants only at their convenience. Only one, or two at the most, hikes could be arranged per week. On each hike a maximum of 10-15 plants could be discovered.

I used three methods to expedite the gathering of data. The first method was the use of colored plates of plants in House's *Book Of Flowers*. This method enjoyed only limited success for several reasons: (1) many of the plants pictured in the book had no local counterpart, (2) many of the flowers pictured are a different species of a locally appearing genus and the small morphological differences caused confusion and, (3) in many cases the plants pictured are idealized, and are all photographed against an artificial background, both causing additional confusion.

The second and third methods were the use of dried plants, shown to the informant for his identification. The plants were either those collected on the reservation (second method) or those brought from the herbarium of the University of Tennessee (third method). In the latter case the specimens were mounted. As a guide to what species should be brought from the University, I used a file supplied to me by Miss Mary Ulma.

The file, compiled by Miss Ulma and Mr. Jess Lambert, listed all plants seen in flower and identified during the spring of 1952.

I first brought 50 herbarium sheets to Cherokee representing the first 50 plants recorded in the file. Many of these plants were unfamiliar to the informants, being of more rare distribution. In the second group, I selected from the remainder of the file some 95 plants which I considered more common to the area. The others were not treated.

The use of dried specimens proved much more successful than the colored plates, although the former method also presented difficulties. Dried plants at best are different from the fresh matter. One of the extreme cases is the delicate Indian pipe *Monotropa uniflora* blooming inconspicuously in a moist bed under the shade of a large tree. In a dried condition it appears as a blackened blob. These last two methods, despite their faults, produced information in quantity and provided an easy way to check the identical plant with more than one informant.

Aggie Lossiah

At first I had no choice but to accept the information given to me in blind faith of its authenticity. Checking later with data from other informants gave some ground for the reliability of information from individual informants, but even more reason for doubt, as many of the usages differed drastically. Still later data indicated there was little hope for even a 50% matching as in most cases each informant had a different use for each plant. This subject is presented more fully in the discussion. I had to revert to blind faith in the gathering of data. It is my opinion, however, that no informant gave false information purposely. Particularly in regard to Yute Jumper, the information gathered is considered absolutely authentic. The data from Aggie Lossiah checked in every detail to the information which she had in the contest entry almost 10 months earlier. Flaws found in this study are human errors; either of the informant misidentifying a plant name or use, or my errors, which we hope are few.

Fourteen persons are considered the main informants of this study, although other individuals have supplied information on a fewer number of plants. In the case of the latter persons, their full name will follow the information attributed to them. In the case of the former 14, their names will be indicated by letters. These persons, the communities in which they live and their initials are listed below.

(1) Aggie and Henry Lossiah, Yellow Hill = A.L.
(2) Tom Lossiah, Soco = T.L.
(3) Noyah Arch, Soco = N.A.
(4) Yute Jumper, Bird Town = Y.J.
(5) Hester Reagon, Jackson County = H.R.
(6) Minnie and Darrel Allison, Bird Town = M.A.
(7) Lillie Hornbuckle, Soco = L.H.
(8) Nancy Conseen, Robbinsville, N. C. = N.C.

(9) Mose Owle, Bird Town = M.O.
(10) Molly Sequoyah, Big Cove = M.S.
(11) Will West Long, Big Cove = W.W.
(12) Cain Screamer, Wolf Town = C.S.

Aggie and Henry Lossiah are taken together. Mr. Lossiah suffered a paralytic stroke three years ago which deprived him of clarity of speech. His English was difficult, if not impossible, to understand and his Cherokee was understood by only a few. Whenever a plant was under consideration, a conversation in Cherokee ensued of which the writer was completely ignorant. After a lively dialogue, Mrs. Lossiah would turn and relate the information. I was never certain who was actually responsible for giving the information, although Aggie confessed ignorance of plant lore. Tom Lossiah is no relation to the latter couple.

Minnie and Darrel Allison are mother and son taken together because of near identical information given by them.

Noyah Arch

I was taken by Aggie and Henry Lossiah to visit Nancy Conseen, a native of Robbinsville, 60 miles from Cherokee.

Of the 14 persons listed, four are white enough to be considered non-Indian, although they have Indian ancestry or relatives. These persons are Minnie and Darrel Allison, Hester Reagon and Lilly Hornbuckle. The discussion section will treat the data gathered from these informants of mixed heritage compared with data from full bloods.

On the suggestion of Mr. John Witthoft, the Cherokee name for the plant was taken along with other data. This later proved highly useful. It provided a further comparison of plants between informants and literature. Moreover, it vouched for the informant's familiarity of the plant under consideration. Each Indian name is annotated as to who supplied it to the writer.

The development of a written language to accompany the spoken language of the Cherokee is one of the extraordinary achievements of all time. In the 1820s a crippled Cherokee of mixed blood observed that the white people had a way of talking on paper. Unaided and in the face of ridicule, he undertook the job of devising a symbol for each Cherokee word or idea. The impossibility of such a system was soon apparent, but in time the ex-hunter discovered that every Cherokee word could be broken down to a limited number of sounds. He improved his first drafts until a system of only 85 sounds was developed. For each of these he devised a symbol which he either invented or borrowed from the English alphabet. He accomplished this in total ignorance of the English language.

So successful was the experiment that almost overnight the Cherokee nation became literate. Anyone who spoke the language could read and write it with little effort. This most famous of all Cherokees is immortalized in the name of North America's oldest living monument, the redwood tree, *Sequoia gigantean,* of California. There are today many living descendants of this famous Cherokee literary character bearing either his name, Sequoyah, or the later family name, Walkingstick.

With the Sequoyah syllabary as a tool, many of the learned medicine men recorded their knowledge concerning Cherokee ceremonies and beliefs. In many of their formulas plant lore is included. I have seen one of these undiscovered manuscripts written and owned by Yute Jumper, and was told by Tom Lossiah of the latter's ownership of one. I regret that the information contained in these two texts remains a secret—a good project for an anthropologist interested in linguistics, or other ethnological studies.

Other manuscripts have been exploited by ethnologists such as James Mooney, Frans Olbrechts, and others. The translation of such material requires the cooperation of an Indian well versed in the use of the syllabary.

A phoneme system has been devised so that any Cherokee word may be written in symbols that can be understood after brief study. This system, outlined below, was suggested to me by John Witthoft.

The phoneme system of Frans Olbrechts, 1932, was not used as it included symbols involving sound distinctions which Cherokees do not recognize. An older phoneme system used by Mahoney, 1849 which is similar to a newer one listed in the Cherokee Fair program (1951), is useless because many fundamental sounds are overlooked.

A great flexibility was noticed in some Cherokee words, especially in the pronunciation of vowels. This will be evidenced later, where it will be seen that the Cherokee names for certain plants fluctuate around a general sound pattern. This is true especially in regard to the several dialects. Again, there are words with slight sound differences having entirely different meanings.

diȟ sti : dance	a˙má : salt
diɬ sti´ : fight	a má : water
ᵈji-yuhʿ: poplar tree or canoe	
ʿsi-yuhʿ: Hello	

It is believed that if the sounds indicated in the phoneme system, above, are carefully duplicated in pronouncing the name of a plant, any Cherokee will understand the speaker's meaning.

In the body of information which is to follow, every plant is listed in a botanical organization: from the plants considered phylogenetically lowest in the plant kingdom to the highest. The plants common name is listed first, then its scientific name (genus, species, authority name). At the end of the description, each plant's Cherokee common name is written phonetically with Cherokee punctuation to make pronunciation possible.

In many cases the Cherokee name is a word having a descriptive significance, such as, "it blows in the wind" for *Baptisia*. Again, the Cherokee name is translatable only to the English common name, as "na t si" for "pine."

The information may be from either an informant or from literature; in either case the source is indicated.

Cherokee Alphabet

D a			ꭶ le			
Ꮪ ga	Ꮕ ka		ꭺ me			
Ꮡ ha			Ꭴ ne			
W la			ꮹ que			
ꭶ ma			4 se			
Ꮎ na	Ꮏ hna	Ꮐ nah	Ꮷ de	Ꮦ te		
Ꮜ qua			L tle			
Ꮀ sa	ꮝ s		Ꮴ tse			
Ꮭ da	W ta		ꮃ we			
Ꮪ dla	Ꮏ tla		β ye			
Ꮟ tsa			T i			
Ꮹ wa			ꭹ gi			

Key To Pronunciation of Cherokee Plant Names

a   as in f<u>a</u>ther

ə   as in the German mädchen (rare)

i   as in m<u>ea</u>t

ı   as in b<u>i</u>t

E   as in f<u>a</u>te

e   as in b<u>a</u>t

d   as an indeterminate vowel sound

ɔc   as in b<u>u</u>t

o   as in r<u>o</u>t

ɔ   as in intermediate between r<u>o</u>t and b<u>ough</u>t

ω   as in b<u>ough</u>t or l<u>a</u>w

u   as in b<u>oo</u>t

SEMI-VOWELS, ACCENTS, ETC.

h   as in <u>h</u>at

y   as in English <u>y</u>ou

w   as in <u>wh</u>ite

·   after a vowel indicates that the vowel is long

(between syllables represents an unvoiced breathed sound. When occuring with an "s," it is expressed as "sh"

?   a glottal catch resembling a hard "k" but sounded more deeply in the throat

,   beneath a vowel represents a nasal quality

´   is the primary accent

`   is the secondary accent

+   first letter is almost silent

CONSONANTS

d, k, l, m, n, s, t, and hard g are as in English

l as in bott<u>le</u> or ratt<u>le</u>

^{d}j as soft g preceded by a d

^{t}s, ^{d}z, and ^{k}l are consonant combinations

Chapter 2

Cherokee Theory and Practice of Medicine

The travelers passing through Indian territory in the 18th and 19th centuries were practically unanimous in their praise of Cherokee medicines and remedies. From the pages of the diaries of these men and women come such favorable testimonies as this one from James Adair, 1775:

> Although the Cherokee showed such little skill in curing the small pox, yet they, as well as all other Indian nations, have a great knowledge of specific virtues in simples; applying herbs and plants, on the most dangerous occasions, and seldom if ever, fail to effect a thorough cure from the natural bush. In the order of nature, every country and climate is blest with specific remedies for the maladies that are connatural to it...the Indians instigated by nature, and quickened by experience, have discovered the peculiar properties of vegetables, as far as needful in their situation of life. For my own part, I would prefer an old Indian before any surgeon whatsoever, in curing green wounds by bullets, arrows, etc. both for the certainty, ease, and speediness of cure; for if those parts of the body are not hurt, which are essential to the preservation of life, they cure the wounded in a trice.

James W. Mahoney, 1849, echoes the above sentiments and writes in the preface of his book, The Cherokee Physician:

> "...Those who will take the pains to read and study, will soon be convinced that the all-wise creator in the infinitude of his mercy, has furnished man with the means of curing his own diseases, in all the climates and countries of which he is an inhabitant."

Mahoney declares in a further burst of faith:

> "The time is not far distant, when most, if not all the diseases of our country, will be healed without the use of calomel and mercurial preparations, and when foreign drugs will be disused by administering physicians."

Many Indians and mountain whites of Cherokee, N. C. still possess confidence in the old-fashioned Indian remedies. There are, of course, those who consult a white physician on occasion, but who will still revert to their ancient medicines.

At least one man who had nothing good to say of the Cherokee remedies was James Mooney. In 1890 he wrote of the Cherokee myth accounting for the origin of some diseases:

> "The white doctor works upon a disordered organism. The Cherokee doctor works to drive out a ghost or a devil. According to the Cherokee myth, disease was invented by the animals in revenge for the injuries inflicted upon them by the human race. The larger animals saw themselves killed and eaten by man, while the smaller animals, reptiles, and insects were trampled upon and wantonly tortured until it seemed that their only hope of safety lay in devising some way to check the increase of mankind. The bears held the first council, but were unable to fix upon any plan of procedure, and dispersed without accomplishing anything. Consequently the hunter never asks pardon of the bear when he kills one. Next the deer assembled and after much discussion invented rheumatism, but decreed at the same time that if the hunter, driven by necessity to kill a deer, should ask its pardon according to a certain formula, he should not be injured. Since then every hunter who has been initiated into the mysteries asks pardon of the slain deer. When this is neglected through ignorance or carelessness, the "Little Deer," the chief of the deer tribe, who can never die or be wounded, tracks the hunter to his home by blood-drops on the ground, and puts the rheumatism spirit into him. Sometimes the hunter, on starting to return to his home, builds a fire in the trail behind him to prevent pursuit by the Little Deer. Later on, councils were held by other animals, birds, fishes, reptiles and insects, each one inventing some new disease to inflict upon humanity, down even to the grubworm, who became so elated at the bright prospect in view that in his joy he sprang into the air, but fell over backward, and had to wriggle on his back, as the grubworm does to this day."

In another paper Mooney, 1885, writes of the promise which the plants make to man:

> "Each tree, shrub and herb, even down to the grasses and mosses, agreed to furnish a remedy for some one of the diseases named, and each said: I shall appear to help man when he calls upon me in his need...When the doctor is in doubt what treatment to apply for the relief of a patient, the spirit of the plant suggests to him the proper remedy."

The old time myths, above, are today forgotten, but the beliefs have survived with certain alterations. Rather than the plants purposely helping man, the Indians believe that:

"when God made this earth, he saw that every plant had a purpose." (Aggie Lossiah)

I asked Mose Owle,
"How did the Indians know what plant to use in case of an illness?"

Mose Owle explained (Paraphrased),

"The old Indians would go to the woods in search of a medicine – they would see a herb over yonder... they would wait until everything was still and quote a verse, a prayer from the Psalms, if the weed shook it was a cure for the disease he was seeking to cure. In seven days the cure would be complete, for God made the earth in seven days."

On being asked the same question, Noyah Arch gave almost the identical answer. The story is definitely related to the story told by Mooney, but with a Christian veneer.

The following outline of Cherokee medicinal beliefs is adapted from Olbrechts, 1932, and Mooney, 1885.

The Treatment of Diseases: the practitioner seeks to attack the cause of the malady. Once it is removed, cure will be effected in four to seven days. Continued illness beyond the seventh day indicates the patient may be suffering from more than one disease. The practitioner discusses with the patient what has happened to him recently in the way of omens, neglected taboos, dreams, etc., to determine the cause.

I. Materia Medica: mostly herbs –

    A. Herbs with a pungent odor are popular medicines.

    B. Some plants are selected from some connection between their appearance and the symptoms of the disease: milkweed for milky urine, etc.

    C. Some plants are selected because the outward appearance suggests a cure, as the unrolling of a fern for rheumatism.

    E. Plants are sometimes thought to possess a peculiar power because of an unusual configuration or growth: a lightning-struck tree, a crippled tree, etc.

II. Preparation of the medicine: four ways of processing plants for use are still known –

    A. Decoction: the plant material is placed in a large amount of water, which is partially boiled away.

    B. Steep: infusion, steep, or "ooze." The plant material is pounded or shredded and is soaked in water, which is usually cold.

    C. Boiled: the plant material is boiled for a short time in water.

    D. Poultice: the plant material, after being treated in one of several ways, is wrapped in cloth and then applied to the ailing spot.

III. Administering of the medicine: usually done by the shaman.

    A. The tea is often drunk. The amount to be taken is rarely specific; "as much as you can hold."

B. In old times the tea was blown on the patient with a blowing tube.

C. For some diseases, the root is simply chewed by the patient.

D. The tea is sometimes applied directly to the ailing spot. In some cases the patient is scratched with a sharpened instrument before the application.

E. A method seldom practiced now is the sweat bath. The medicine is poured over heated stones while the patient inhales the fumes. In earlier times this treatment was associated with a sweat house: in later times the patient wrapped himself up in a blanket and lay on his bed. Sweating was followed by a plunge in cold water.

IV. Formulas: see Chapter 5.

In addition to treatment of disease with herb medicines and formulas, various physical means were employed. These include "going to the water" and divination with beads.

In general there are two types of practitioners: the herbalist and the conjurer. There is a real distinction between the two, although a single person may lay claim to being both.

The herbalist is an Indian man or woman who has workable knowledge of herbs and their uses. He will treat a person who comes to him without charge although he may accept a gift; he criticizes the white physician who charges a fee.

"You see, white doctors are out after money. We will help a sick man...and if he recovers we are glad. But your doctors, if they do not get money, they will not cure. So they make healthy people ill on purpose, that they may cure them and get rich." * The herbalist declares emphatically that he is not a medicine man, and uses only herbs in his cure.

The divinator, or medicine man, partook in ballgame preliminaries and the Green Corn Ceremony. He used witchcraft as well as plants, and exacted a fee for his services. He sometimes used his magic to harm people.

---

* Not an actual quotation, this is the expressed sentiment of Yute Jumper.

Plants Used by Eastern Cherokee Indians

Non-Vascular Plants

MUSHROOM FAMILY *Fungi*

Puffball
Lycoperdon pyriforme Persoon

(1) The dried spores are used as a powder on old sores (A. L.).

No kwi si usdi gidↄ́, *(Olbrecht, 1932), (Cherokee names probably applicable to all "puffballs.")*

Puffball
Geaster spp.

(1) The dried spores are used as a powder to make the funiculus fall off a newborn child (W. W.).

Beefsteak Mushroom
Fistulina hepatica Fr.

(1) This mushroom, when eaten, has the taste of beef (Jess Lambert, W. W.).

ALGAE FAMILY *Algae*

Blue-green Algae

(1) Blue-green algae from stagnant water is used in a poultice to cure a headache (W. W.).

LICHEN FAMILY *Lichens*

Fruticose Lichens

(1) Several types of fruticose lichen "pot scrapings" are collected from off fallen stems and are used for cancer medicine (Mooney, Ms.).

U ^{t_s}alEla, *(W. W.).*

Vascular Plants

ADDER'S TONGUE FAMILY *Ophioglossaceae*

Rattlesnake Fern
Botrychium virginianum (L.) Sw.

(1) The root is used as an alternate ingredient in the medicine accompanying Formula 5: "For dreaming of snakes."

UsÈli·t i (*(Olbrecht, 1932) "it held erect."*

ROYAL FERN FAMILY *Osmundaceae*

Cinnamon Fern
Osmunda cinnamomea (L.)

(1) The entire plant is used as as ingredient in the medicine accompanying Formula 41: "For chills."

Igɔliuwɔ·skili ustiga, *(Olbrecht, 1932).*

FERN FAMILY *Polypodiaceae*

Maidenhair Fern
Adiantum pedatum (L.)

(1) The entire plant is used as an ingredient in the medicine accompanying Formula 41: "For chills." (2) A decoction of the whole plant is used as an emetic in case of ague and fever (Witthoft,1947b). (3) A tea made by pouring boiling water over the leaves is used for rheumatism; another fern is also used (Mooney, Ms.). *...The doctors explained that the fronds of the different varieties of fern are curled up in the young plant, but unroll and straighten out as it grows, and consequently a decoction of ferns causes the contracted muscles of the rheumatic patient to unbend and straighten out in like manner...* (Mooney, 1885). (4) A leaf tea is drunk and used as a wash to cure fevers (Mooney, Ms.). (5) The powdered leaves, when smoked, are good for heart trouble (M. A.). (6) For sudden paralytic attack, as in bad pneumonia of children, a steep of the entire plant is blown all over the head and chest of the patient, where he is hot. A prayer is said (W. W.).

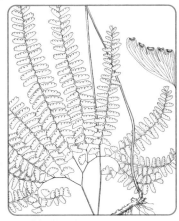

Kogú skedɑgE, *(W. W.),* KɔgɑsasgudɑgÉ, *(W. W.), "it held erect,"* Kaku, *(W. W.).*

Walking Fern
Asplenium rhizophyllum (L.) Link

(1) An ingredient of the medicine accompanying Formula 29: "When their breast swells."
(2) Those who dream of snakes drink a decoction of this fern and *Hepatica acutiloba* to produce vomiting, after which the dreams do not return (W. W.).

Logwis'i, *(C. S.), "star,"* Inatugan'Ká, *(Olbrecht, 1932), "snake tongue."*

Fragile Fern
Cystopteris fragilis (L.) Bernh.

(1) An ingredient of the medicine accompanying Formula 41: "For chills."

Igɔli uwɔ·skili noyɔi'Ei, *(Olbrecht, 1932).*

Hay-scented Fern
Dennstaedtia punctilobula (Michx.) Moore

(1) An ingredient of the medicine accompanying Formula 41: "For chills."

IgɔliuyEla'ɔ, *(Olbrecht, 1932).*

Wood-Fern
Dryopteris spp.

(1) A root decoction is drunk to produce vomiting (Mooney, 1885). (2) A root decoction, sometimes with other plants added, is rubbed on the skin for rheumatism after preliminary scratching (Ibid). (3) A warm decoction is held in the mouth to relieve toothache (Ibid).

Yaná u'Está, *(Mooney, 1885).*

Christmas Fern
Polystichum acrostichoides (Michx.) Schott

(1) An ingredient of the medicine accompanying Formula 41: "For chills." (2) A tea of the leaves is rubbed on for indigestion (A. L.). (3) A cold water infusion of the roots is drunk by old folks for stomachache or bowel complaint (N. A.).

Christmas Fern
Polystichum acrostichoides

Gig∝gÉ ugwaguwindi^{dz}u,́ *(W. W.), "red on inside of leaves,"* Yɔ·nəu^{dz}E·stɔ,́ *(Olbrecht, 1932),* Yɔn∝u^{dj}Estɔ,́ *(Olbrecht, 1932), "bear's bed,"* Galí, *(A. L.).*

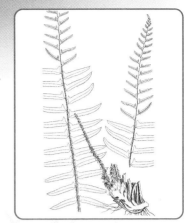

PINE FAMILY *Pinaceae*

Spruce
Picea rubens Sarg.

(1) The bark is used in modern basketry (Wilson Reed).

Short Leaf Pine
Pinus echinata Mill.

(1) A tea of the needles is taken for coughs and "hang on" (M. A.).

Nɔ^{ts}i,́ *(A. L., W. W.), "pine."*

Table Mountain Pine
Pinus pungens Lamb.

(1) A decoction including the cone of a yellow pine tree, the stem of *Impatiens capensis*, the root of *Veronica officinalis*, and the bark of *Ulmus rubra* is given to pregnant women before going to the water each new moon. The pine is used because it represents the quality of long life and unimpaired health, which will be given to the offspring (Olbrecht, 1932).

Nɔ^{ts}i,́ *(W. W.), "pine."*

Virginia Pine
Pinus virginiana Mill.

(1) Used in the medicine accompanying Formula 12: "For an incantation disease caused by

Virginia Pine
Pinus virginiana

a maligning conjuror." (2) A root tea is used for sore throat (Minnie Saunooke). (3) The root is boiled in a tub, the turpentine is skimmed off, and the solution is spread on a tanned deer's skin for a drawing plaster (Witthoft, 1947b). (4) The needles are used in modern basketry (Wilson Reed). (5) A bunch of "buds" (two-inch-long stem tips) with the needles are made into a tea (boiling is optional) which is used to check bowels or stop coughing (A. L.). (6) Pine branches are burned in cooking vessels and the ashes are thrown on the rekindled hearth fire in a home after a death for purification. This is sometimes done also in the house of the relatives (Olbrecht, 1932). (7) The needles of pine, the bark of *Hamamelis virginiana,* and *Lindera benzoin* are made into a hot tea decoction (boiling five or ten minutes). The patient drinks the tea, covers up, and his fever "breaks out." (T. L.) (8) The needles of pine and the stem of *Vicia caroliniana* are put in a bucket with apple juice and drunk by the ballplayers for wind during the game. (N. A.) (9) A person with a cold may wrap himself in blankets and steam his room with boiling water in which pine needles have been dropped. (H. R.) (10) The needles or the gum of pine (or the root of Sassafras) was used in the old days to flavor homemade soap.* (A. L.) (11) The roots of pine, *Rubus trivialis* and *Alnus serrulata* (a handful of each), are made into a tea which is good for piles. The tea is drunk and used as a bath. (A. L.)

Nɔ̆ts.ı́, *(A. L., W. W.), "pine."*

* When A. L. was a young woman the practice of her family was to collect the ashes from all fires throughout the year, saving them in a hopper kept for that purpose. In the spring, when the hogs were slaughtered, the soap was made. The ashes were soaked in water and the lye drippings were collected in a cooking vessel. The strength of the lye was cut by the addition of hog lard. The lye and lard were cooked for the length of time necessary to give the hardness of soap desired. The writer has used a fine quality soap of this kind made by Mandy Walkingstick.

Hemlock
Tsuga canadensis (L.) Carr.

(1) A tea made of the stem tips of hemlock is used for kidney trouble (A. L.). (2) Hemlock bark is pounded and used in a poultice for itching armpits (W. W.). (3) A decoction including hemlock, *Smilax glauca* and *Platanus occidentalis* is drunk to expel afterbirth (Olbrecht, 1932). (3) The bark is used in modern basketry (Wilson Reed). (5) The bark is made into a rose-tan fabric dye (Leftwich, 1952).

Nɔnu, *(W. W.), "hemlock."*

WATER PLANTAIN FAMILY *Alismataceae*

Arrowhead
Sagittaria latifolia Willd.

(1) If a baby fevers too much, bathe it in a tea made of the leaves. Also give them one sip (A. L.). (2) A witch's potion (Olbrecht, 1932).

KɑnE·?si, *(T. L.)*,

Aɔli lEɔski, *(Olbrecht, 1932)*.

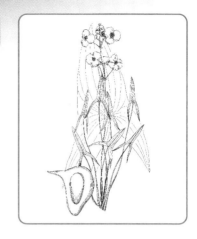

GRASS FAMILY *Poaceae*

Beardgrass, Broomsedge
Andropogon virginicus (L.)

(1) An ingredient in a green corn medicine with *Impatiens spp.*, *Zea Mays,* and *Cucurbita pepo* (M. S.). In a second green corn medicine (see Appendix) it is one of three required ingredients (W. W.). (2) Of magical significance with the recitation of Formula 60: "For prevention or cure of frostbitten feet." (3) A tea of the entire plant is used to bathe the sores caused by poison oak (M. A.). (4) One of the ingredients which is mixed with mutton tallow, making a salve for sores (M. A.). (5) The stems are used in a yellow dye for fabrics (Leftwich, 1952). (6) The tops, when in solution with onion peels, make a dye ranging from yellow to orange (M. A.).

KɑnEskɑwɔ·di, *(Olbrecht, 1932),* SE lu Kwayɑ, *(W. W.).*

Small Cane
Arundinaria tecta (Walt.) Muhl.

(1) Used in aboriginal as well as contemporary basketry (see Appendix) (Speck, 1920).

I⟨ya, *(Speck 1920), "cane."*

Giant Cane
Arundinaria gigantea (Walt.) Chapm.

(1) Used in aboriginal as well as contemporary basketry (Ibid). (2) The stalks are used for

Giant Cane
Arundinaria gigantea

blowguns. The joints are heated over a fire and the tube is straightened (John Witthoft).

I'ya, *(Speck 1920), "cane."*

Job's Tears
Coix Lacryma-Jobi (L.)

(1) The seeds are strung around the baby's neck for teething (T. L.). "A universal custom of Mediterranean origin" (John Witthoft).

Se lu u ni dz i, *(M. S.), "corn, their mother." (Introduced)*

Panic Grass
Panicum spp.

(1) The stems are used for padding the inside of moccasins (T. L.).

Ka nE·sq∝, *(T. L.).*

Corn, Volunteer Corn
Zea mays (L.)

(1) Corn is the major economic crop of the Cherokee Indians. (2) Volunteer corn is an ingredient in a green corn medicine with *Andropogon virginicus, Impatiens spp.* and *Cucurbita pepo* (M. S.). In a second green corn medicine (see Appendix), volunteer corn is an alternate ingredient (W. W.). The exposed buttress of a corn stalk is used in a green corn medicine (N. C.).

Se lu *(N. C., A. L.), "corn,"* Se lu g∝wat∝, *(M. S.), "corn wild,"* ∝wo sa·ul si yEnEhi, *(W. W.) "it came up by itself."*

Cotton Grass
Eriophorum spp.

(1) The plant has some use in medicine with a prayer, but not by W. W. (W. W.).

dj is +u ski d∝ti, *(W. W.), "rabbit's tail."*

Great Bulrush
Scirpus validus Vahl.

(1) An ingredient in the medicine accompanying formula 20: "For spoiled saliva." (2) The great bulrush is one of the few herbs which is cultivated by medicine men (Olbrecht, 1932).

Gɔnɔga⁺su·t⁶n⁽ʼ⁽, *(Olbrecht, 1932).*

ARUM FAMILY *Araceae*

Sweetflag, Calamus
Acorus calamus (L.)

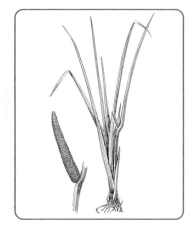

(1) An ingredient in the medicine accompanying Formula 80: "For itching privates..." (N. A., W. W.). (2) The root is chewed for colds, headache and sore throat (M. A.). (3) A hot root infusion, when drunk, is good for colds (N. A.).

U⁽yɔdɔli, *(Olbrecht, 1932),* Us ti ga gɔ dusE , *(Olbrecht, 1932).*

Jack-in-the-pulpit
Arisaema triphyllum (L.) Schott

(1) The root is beaten and used in a poultice for boils "before they run." "The roots look as though covered with boils" (M. S.). (2) Several of the roots (which look like a boil) are roasted in coals for two or three seconds. The roots are then cut into pieces the size of "possum grapes" and rolled into balls. For kidney trouble eat 2, 3, 4, or 7 of the balls (W. W.). (3) The root is made into a poultice which is used for headache (A. L.).

Tu`s⁽ti, *(T. L., N. A.),* Tu`ˢti, *(W. W.),*
Tu yas ti, *(M. S.),* Yɔdɔgwɔ lɔ·ski, *(A. L.).*

Golden Club
Orontium aquaticum (L.)

(1) The root is crushed and used in a poultice for muscle soreness after scratching the afflicted area. When Mandy Walkingstick was a young girl the plant was grown in springs near the cabins because of its scarcity in the area (M. W.). (2) A steep is prepared in which children bathe every new moon to ward off epidemic disease: whooping cough, measles,

Golden Club
Orontium aquaticum

etc. (W. W.). (3) Babies are bathed in a steep to give them strength (Olbrecht, 1932).

Ga nE·s, *(W. W.)*, KɔnEsi, *(Olbrecht, 1932).*

YELLOW-EYED GRASS FAMILY *Xyridaceae*

Yellow-eyed Grass
Xyris caroliniana Walt.

(1) A root steep is drunk for diarrhea, when the stools are liquid and yellow in color. Especially good for children. *Sisyrinchium* may be used instead (W. W.).

Da lo ni gÉ, *(W. W.)*, nas t E^{dz}i.

SPIDERWORT FAMILY *Commelinaceae*

Spiderwort
Tradescantia virginiana (L.)

(1) The young plant is eaten in salads or as greens in the spring (T. L., A. L., N. A., Witthoft, 1947b). (2-3) A tea of spiderwort and six other ingredients is drunk for female ailments, or for "rupture" (M. S.). (4) Spiderwort is one of the ingredients in a medicine for kidney trouble, a prayer is necessary (W. W.). (5) When a person craves some food and eats too much, beat up the root of spiderwort and make a tea. The sore stomach will be cured when the tea is drunk (A. L.). (6) A poultice of the beaten roots will cure cancer (Lottie May Squirrel).

Ta g wa ló, *(M. S.)*, Tɔgwɔ·li, *(A. L., N. A.)*,

Tɔgwa·lɔ, *(W. W.)*, Yo nủ ni gi sti, "spiderwort, *(C. S.)*, (beargrass).

RUSH FAMILY *Juncaceae*

Wire Grass
Juncus tenuis Willd.

(1) The tea of wire grass is a ballplayer medicine. The sturdy character of its stems keeps the player from falling down (Sevier Crowe). (2) Babies are washed in the tea of wire grass to ensure strength in growing up (M. O.). A tea of wire grass and common plantain, *Plantago spp.*, is given to an infant when first starting to crawl or walk to prevent lameness (Y. J.).

Ka nEskaᴂ, *(M. S.), "grass,"* Nᴂnɔu dEdɔ?tí, *(Y. J.).*

Soft Rush
Juncus effusus (L.)

(1) An ingredient in the medicine accompanying Formula 20: "For spoiled saliva caused by dreaming of snakes."

Gᴂna gá us ti gá, *(Olbrecht, 1932).*

Rush
Juncus spp.

(1) Several species of rush are used as string in binding up dough in oak leaves for cooking bread (A. L.).

LILY FAMILY *Liliaceae*

Fly Poison
Amianthium muscitoxicum (Walt.) Gray

(1) The root is a crow poison and a sure, but severe, cure for the itch (Witthoft, 1947b).

Trout Lily, Dog's Tooth Violet
Erythronium americanum Ker

(1) A root tea will break a fever (A. L.). (2) Warm the leaves over a fire, crush them in your hand, and pour the juice over a wound that won't heal (C. S.). (3) Beat the roots of dog's tooth violet and *Panax trifolius* and make a cold infusion which is good for fainting persons (Y. J.). (4) When "mountain trout" blooms it is time to fish. Chew the root and spit them into the river when you go fishing to make the fish bite "because it is marked like trout" (M. S.).

Trout Lily, Dog's Tooth Violet
Erythronium americanum

An ɔt⁺saʹ, *(A. L.)*, Adɔsiʹ, *(C. S.)*, Ad ɔ⁺saʹ,
(Y. J.), Adɔn saʹ, *(M. S.)*, "trout," "mountain trout."

Narrow Leaved Plantain Lily
Hosta japonica (Thumb.) Voss

(1) Steep the leaves (don't boil), rub the tea on swollen parts of the leg and feet caused by invisible insects. Scratch the sore parts before applying and use the medicine with a formula (W. W.). (2) When you cough and spit blood, make a warm infusion of the roots taken from the east side of the plant (Source unknown).

^{dz}ɔ·stɔ·nis ti, *"whipping with a small stick,"* Gɔ·stɔ·ni stiʹ, *(W. W.). (Introduced)*

Turk's Cap Lily
Lilium superbum (L.)

(1) For flux (loose and bloody stool), drink a warm or cold root infusion (N. A.). (2) A root decoction is given to infants to drink and be bathed in to make them fleshy and fat (from the fleshy character of the roots, Olbrecht, 1932). (3) A thick root decoction is used as a lotion to rub on rheumatic joints (A. L.). (4) The root is beaten into flour which can be used in making bread (N. C.).

Kan gu^{dz}ɔtaʹ, *(W. W.)*, Kɔni gu⁺sɔtiʹ,
(Olbrecht, 1932), Kal sto·gaʹ, *(M. S.)*,
Kan gu^{dj}ɔtaʹ, *"lily."*

Wild Yellow Lily
Lilium canadense (L.)

The writer believes that this lily and *L. superbum* are confused by most Indians and that the Cherokee names and usages above probably apply to both species. One usage may be confined to this species: (1) Boil the roots of wild yellow lily and wild orange-red lily into a decoction and apply to rheumatic joints (M. S.).

Wild Orange-red Lily
Lilium spp.

(1) Boil the roots of wild orange-red lily and *L. canadense* into a decoction and apply to rheumatic joints (M. S.). (2) The root of wild orange-red lily is boiled and prepared like hominy and eaten in famine times. (The root resembles an ear of corn) (W. W.).

Ga^{ha}gu sà ta gĭ, *(W. W.).*

Solomon's Seal
Polygonatum biflorum (Walt.) Ell.

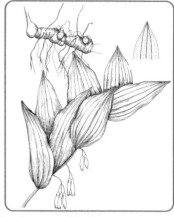

(1) The young leaves are eaten in the spring in a number of ways: raw, boiled, or boiled and fried. They may be eaten either in a salad or as greens (N. A., A. L., Y. J., T. L.). (2) A long time ago, the roots were dried and beaten and used as flour for bread (Mandy Walkingstick, Y. J.). (3) The roots can be ground and used as salt (M. S.). (4) The root is heated and bruised and applied as a poultice to remove ulcerated swelling resembling a boil or carbuncle (Mooney, 1885). (5) The root when roasted, beaten up, and made into a tea is a good medicine for stomach trouble (N. C.). (6) A medicine of solomon's seal is taken for "spoiled saliva," caused by dreaming of the dead, making the patient feel exhausted. Take the root and some dirt from in front of a groundhog's den that came from far underground, and boil the two in a gallon or more of water. "Drink as much as you can and make yourself vomit it up with your finger until you cannot throw up any more, for four straight mornings" (W. W.).

U ga nas ta, *(A. L., N. C., Mandy Walkingstick),* U ta nas ta, *(M. S.),* "sweet," Wal^{ɔ}sun^{ɑ} l stĭ, *(W. W.), "frog fighting."*

False Solomon's Seal
Maianthemum racemosa (L.) Desf.

(1) Steep the root in cold water, bathe sore eyes in it (M. S.).

U dil stĭ, *(N. C.).*

Sawbrier
Smilax glauca (Walt.)

(1) The roots of sawbrier, *Platanus occidentalis* and *Tsuga caroliniana* are boiled into a decoction which is drunk to expel afterbirth. The roots from all the plants must be gathered from the east side of the plant (Olbrecht, 1932). (2) The patient is scratched with the stem of sawbrier in Formula 19: "For rheumatism." (3) An ingredient in the medicine accompanying Formula 28: "For local pains, cramps, and twitchings, etc. caused by dreaming of animals." (4) Apply the wilted leaves to a boil to bring it to a head, or to

Sawbrier
Smilax glauca

open sores to draw out the pus (H. R.). (5) For "bad disease" drink a tea made by boiling for a short time the bark of sawbrier, *Euonymus americanus, Liquidambar styraciflua, Vitis aestivalis, Platanus occidentalis, Fagus grandifolia,* and *Nyssa sylvatica* (T. L.).

G∝ᵈliwɔ·di, *(Olbrecht, 1932), "he climbs down,"*
Nu gu i, *(Olbrecht, 1932),* ªNu ga⁺l∝, *(T. L.),*
"brier."

Carrion Flower
Smilax herbacea (L.)

(1) The vines and roots of carrion flower and *S. rotundifolia*, when boiled together is a tea good for any stomach trouble. A prayer is sometimes said (W. W.).

Sik∝ti∝ski, *(W. W.), "grows just one day."*

Common Greenbrier
Smilax rotundifolia (L.)

(1) (See *S. herbacea*, above.)

Ani ski na un∝ne sad∝, *(W. W.), "for the leg."*

Twisted Stalk
Streptopus roseus Michx.

(1) The young leaves are collected in the spring and eaten in several ways: by itself, with *Polygonatum biflorum*, or with beans (N. C., A. L., T. L.). They say that a frog and a snake got in a fight. The frog got away from the snake by hiding under this weed (Henry Lossiah).

W∝lɔsi u∝l sti, *(A. L.), "frog fight,"* ᵈᶻu li ski, *(A. L.),* ᵈᶻu hil gi, *(N. C.).*

Trillium (all species)

(1) This plant is in some way associated with the myth of SELu (see Appendix, Green Corn Ceremony). The plant is not used for medicine. At least six informants gave the name, but no use for the plant (Y. J., A. L., T. L., M. S., N. A., N. C.). "...They are not picked or used for anything. These flowers are just like people and the thunders play with them" (M. S.).

Ay∝di gwalɔski, *(A. L., T. L., N. A., N. C.),* A yud∝gw∝lo ski, *(W. W.),*
∝niˡyad∝gwalɔski, *(M. S.), "thunder and lightning."*

Wild Oats
Uvularia sessilifolia (L.)

(1) The smashed root is made into a steep which is drunk for diarrhea (M. S.).

Wa lu si´ u⁽u ga´, *(M. S.),* ᵈᶻus ga´ da lŏ·di´, *(M. S.).*

False Hellbore
Veratrum viride Ait.

(1) Used in the medicines accompanying Formula 31: "For soreness in the muscles." Used in the medicine accompanying Formula 36: "For shifting pains."

A·is kw∝nE·d´ɔ, *(Olbrecht, 1932).*

Adam's Needle
Yucca filamentosa (L.)

(1) In a green corn medicine (see Appendix) Adam's needle is a required ingredient. (2) The root or leaves (or both) are boiled into a tea which is drunk for sugar diabetes (W. W.). (3) The roots when pounded and boiled can be used as a soap to wash blankets, etc. (4) To intoxicate fishes, by strewing them pounded on the water (Witthoft, 1947b).

Se lu kwo ya´, *(W. W.).*

AMARYLLIS FAMILY *Agavaceae*

False Aloe
Agave virginica (L.)

(1) The root is chewed in obstinate cases of diarrhea with wonderful success. It is however, a very strong medicine (Witthoft, 1947b).

IRIS FAMILY *Iridaceae*

Blue-eyed Grass
Sisyrinchium spp.

(1) A root steep is drunk for diarrhea, when the stools are liquid and yellow in color. Especially good for children. *Xyris caroliniana* may be used instead (W. W.). (2) Eaten in salads (N. A.).

Da lo ni´ gÉ nas tEᵈᶻ i´, *(W. W.), "yellow root,"* E gwa´ u lis⁽i´, *(N. A.), "grandchild."*

ORCHID FAMILY *Orchidaceae*

Putty Root, Adam and Eve
Aplectrum hyemale (Muhl.) Torr.

(1) The root is used in medicine to make children fleshy and fat (Olbrecht, 1932). (2) The roots are put in slop to make the hogs fat (A. L.).

Putty Root, Adam and Eve
Aplectrum hyemale

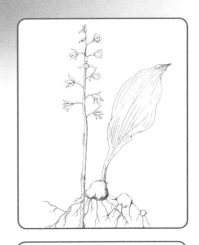

Pink Lady's Slipper
Cypripedium acaule Ait.

(1) A tea of pink lady's slipper and *C. calceolus var. pubescens* is drunk for sugar diabetes (W. W.). (2) A strong tea of pink lady's slipper and *Sanicula spp.* is drunk for stomach cramps (A. L.). (3) A warm steep of the roots of pink lady's slipper and *Comandra umbellata* is drunk for kidney trouble (M. S.). (4) A hot tea made of four entire plants will relieve rupture pains in either men or women (H. R.). (5) Root tea will relieve the pains of female monthly trouble and "change of life" (H. R.). (6) A root tea is good for kidneys and nerves (N. A.)

U sti skwEun la sulɔ́ɔ, *(T. L.),*
ʔKwE^hi u la sulɔ h´^i, *(N. A.),* ʔGw u lasʕu láʹ, *(A. L.), "lady slipper."*

Large Yellow Lady's Slipper
Cypripedium calceolus L. var. parviflorum (Salisb.) Fern.

(1) For colds or stomach ache, beat up the roots, make a cold tea and drink (N. A.). (2) An ingredient in the medicine accompanying Formula 52: "For removing worms." (3) To break a high fever, drink a hot root tea and cover up (N. C.). (4) Decoction of the root used for worms in children. In the liquid is placed some stalks of the common chickweed, or purslane *(Cerastium vulgatum)* which, from the appearance of its red, fleshy stalks, is supposed to have some connection with worms (Mooney, 1885). (5) A hot root tea is good

for nerves, flu, colds, and neuralgia (M. A.). (6) Boil the roots of the three kinds of lady's slipper (small purple, large yellow, and small yellow) into a tea for sugar diabetes (W. W.).

Gwa la sulœ, *(A. L.),* Ko?kwEu na la sulœ, *(A. L.), "partridge moccasin."*

Small Yellow Lady's Slipper
Cypripedium calceolus L. var pubescens (Willd.) Correll

(1) A tea of small yellow lady's slipper and *C. acaule* is drunk for sugar diabetes (see also part 6, above) (W. W.).

Rattlesnake Plantain
Goodyera pubescens (Willd.) R. Br.

(1) For relief of toothache, beat the roots fine and make a tea. Hold the tea in mouth (N. A.). (2) A cold tea of the leaves is good for colds, kidneys, and will improve the appetite (used with whiskey) (H. R.). (3) Soak the plant in water and drip the ooze in sore eyes (Sevier Crowe). (4) A decoction of rattlesnake plantain, *Alnus serrulata, Prunus serotina, Asarum canadense,* and *Xanthorhiza simplicissima* is a good blood tonic. "Take several swallows before a meal... builds the appetite" (M. A.).

Igœ ʰᵃli, *(N. A.).*

Yellow Fringed Orchis
Platanthera ciliaris (L.) R. Br.

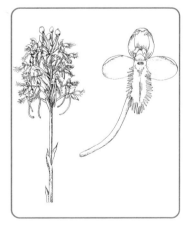

(1) A cold "root" (rhizome) infusion will relieve headache (A. L.). (2) Put a piece of the "root" on a fish-hook to make the fish bite better (W. W.). (3) A warm tea infusion drunk every hour will check the flux (N. C.).

U gu ku us ka, *(A. L.), "owl's head,"*
A⁺sa ti a ni·gwœ·tœ, *(W. W.), "fish strung on a stick,"* U ko?kwÉu na la su·lœ, *(M. S.),*
"bobwhite's moccasin."

Yellow Twayblade
Liparis loeselii (L.) Richard

(1) Boil the roots of yellow twayblade and *Spiranthes lucida.* Drink this tea when the urine is sharp and clear and it hurts to urinate (W. W.).

Uyᵓda li yu sti, *(W. W.).*

Ladies' Tresses
Spiranthes lucida (H. H. Eat.) Ames

(1) Wash infant in a warm steep to ensure fast, healthy growth (N. C.). (2) For urinary trouble (see *Liparis loeselii,* above).

Glad∝skatɔnk´∝, *(A. L.), (W. W.).*

LIZARD'S-TAIL FAMILY *Saururaceae*

Lizard's-tail
Saururus cernuus (L.)

(1) The roots are roasted and mashed and used in poultices (Witthoft, 1947b).

WILLOW FAMILY *Salicaceae*

Willow
Salix spp.

(1) The bark of several species is used in modern basketry (Leftwich, 1952).

White Willow
Salix alba (L.)

(1) An ingredient in the medicine accompanying Formula 21: "For aggravated hoarseness." (2) The stripped twigs are used in basketry (Wilson Reed).

Di lig∝li ski´egwɔ, *(Olbrecht, 1932), "willow big,"* Tsi ga li´a, *(W. W.), "willow." (Introduced)*

Mountain Willow
Salix humilis Marsh.

(1) The root is chewed for hoarseness (A. L.). (2) Pieces of the root are chewed by the ballplayers before and during the game. Water must not be drunk. This is good to give extra wind (N. A., A. L.).

Di la ga lis gi´, *(A. L., N. A.),* Di l∝g lis´ki´, *(T. L.).*

WALNUT FAMILY *Juglandaceae*

Hickory
Carya spp. (L.)

(1) In basketry, strips of hickory bark are used to finish the rim (Speck, 1920). (2) A bark steep is drunk by ballplayers before the game to make the limbs more supple (N. A.). (3) An infusion drunk for the cure of a type of tuberculosis caused by incantation includes the barks of hickory, *Castanea dentata, Fagus grandifolia, Quercus spp., Liriodendron tulipifera,* and *Tilia spp.* (W. W.). (4) For relief of the pain of poliomyelitis. Bark of a black hickory tree is beaten and allowed to soak in old water. The infusion is put in the mouth and blown on the afflicted spots. "The pain leaves like magic, but the patient is left crip-

pled" (M. O.). (5) Chew the leaves of hickory and the whole flower of a giant sunflower and you spit the color of blood. This might be used as a dye (W. W.).

^aW∝nÉ, *(Olbrecht, 1932),* Wa nE⁽i, *(W. W.).*

Mockernut Hickory
Carya tomentosa Nutt.

(1) Used in the medicine accompanying Formula 61: For "thrash." (2) Used in the medicine accompanying Formula 69: "For shot and arrow wounds." (3) The straightened branches are used for the making of arrows (M. O.).

^uW∝nÉ⁽?, *(M. O.),* ^uWa nÉ, *(Olbrecht, 1932, "hickory."*

Butternut
Juglans cinerea (L).

(1) For toothache, make a warm or cold infusion of several barks: butternut, *Prunus serotina, Diospyros virginiana,* and *Alnus serrulata.* "Hold the tea in your mouth against the decayed tooth, and the pus will come to a head" (N. A.). (2) A black splint dye is made of the bark (Nancy Long, Leftwich, 1952). A rich brown dye is made of the bark (M. A.). (3) "A kind of pills are prepared from the inner bark and used as a cathartic" (Witthoft, 1947b).

Ko há, *(M. O.), "butternut,"* Há ya gi da, *(N. A.).*

Black Walnut
Juglans nigra (L.)

(1) A taboo is placed on the eating of black walnuts by pregnant women, or the child will have a broad nose (Olbrecht, 1932). (2) The bark is not used in medicines because it is too poisonous (W. W.). (3) A hot infusion of the inner bark is drunk for smallpox (Lloyd Lambert). (4) The bark of black walnut is a well-known stain (Speck, 1920, A. L., Leftwich, 1952, N. A., etc.). (5) The bark is strewn in streams to poison the fish (W. W.).

Black Walnut
Juglans nigra

Se di, *(W. W.)*, Se ti, *(W. W.)*, *"black walnut."*

BIRCH FAMILY *Betulaceae*

Alder
Alnus spp. (W. W.)

(1) Used in the medicine accompanying Formula 9: "For sore eyes caused by dreaming of a rattlesnake." (2) An ingredient in the medicine accompanying Formula 33: "For pain in different places." (3) An ingredient in the medicine accompanying Formula 34: "For vomiting when the stomach is yellow." (4) Used in the medicine accompanying Formula 35: "For sore eyes." (5) An ingredient in the medicine accompanying Formula 51: "For menstruating women who dream of giving birth to animals or unnatural beings." (6) Used in the medicine accompanying Formula 58: "For disease caused by magically introduced objects." (7) For milky urine. (8) For sore eyes. A bark infusion of speckled alder and *Alnus serrulata* is rubbed and blown into the eyes of the patient, repeating two or four times (Source unknown). (9) One of the plants cultivated by medicine men (Olbrecht, 1932). (10) A bark infusion is drunk for heart trouble (H. R.).

∝(tↄ⁺aE i, *(W. W.)*, Ots E i, *(Olbrecht, 1932)*, *"alder."*

Common Alder
Alnus serrulata (Ait.) Willd.

(1) An ingredient in the medicine accompanying Formula 33: "For pain in different places." (2) An ingredient in the medicine accompanying Formula 86: "For indigestion." (3) For sore eyes (see part 7 of *Alnus rugosa*). (4) A hot berry tea is for high fevers. The patient wraps himself in a blanket and sweats (T. L.). (5) A bark steep is drunk for coughs (T. L.). A cold tea of bark scrapings makes the kidneys act (Lloyd Lambert). (7) Alder bark tea is given to newborn for "thrush," a soreness of the mouth (M. O.). (8) For toothache, make a warm or cold infusion of several barks: alder, *Juglans cinerea*, *Diospyros virginiana* and *Prunus serotina*. "Hold the tea in your mouth against the decayed tooth, and the pus will come to a head" (N. A.). (9) The roots of alder, *Pinus virginiana* and *Rubus trivialis* (a

36

handful of each), are made into a tea which is good for piles. The tea is drunk and used as a bath (A. L.). (10) Skin the bark and make a cold water infusion. This tea is good to purify the blood or bring down high blood pressure (H. R.). (11) A warm bark tea when drunk will check "excessive bleeding" of females (A. L.). (12) A decoction of alder, *Prunus serotina, Goodyera pubescens, Asarum canadense,* and *Xanthorhiza simplicissima* is a good blood tonic. "Take several swallows before a meal... builds the appetite" (M. A.). (13) A bark decoction of alder alone is a general tonic (M. A.).

It sEi, *(Olbrecht, 1932),* AD⊃ ^dj^EHi, *(A. L.),* S ^dj^E hi, *(N. A.).*

Sweet Birch
Betula lenta (L.)

(1) A young man being initiated into the profession of medicine man will, when in danger of coming into contact with a menstrual woman, chew a piece of the inner bark and spit "where his soul lies." His magical powers are otherwise in jeopardy (Olbrecht, 1932). (2) A bark infusion is taken for the stomach (A. L.).

∝⁺so ni, *(Olbrecht, 1932), "birch."*

River Birch
Betula nigra (L.)

(1) An ingredient in the medicine accompanying Formula 22: "For milky urine." (2) A tea is made of bark sap which is drunk to check the bowels (H. R.).

Ga nE ti skin⊃, *(W. W.),* G∝nEtis gi, *(Olbrecht, 1932), "birch."*

American Hornbeam
Carpinus caroliniana Walt.

(1) An ingredient in the medicine accompanying Formula 22: "For milky urine." (2) Used in the medicine accompanying Formula 65: "For navel yellowness."

tsu·ti na, *(Olbrecht, 1932), "hornbeam."*

Hazelnut
Corylus americana Walt.

(1) An ingredient in the medicine accompanying Formula 34: "For when the stomach is yellow."

U yu gi da, *(Olbrecht, 1932),* Ha yu gi da, *(N. A.).*

Ironwood
Ostrya virginiana (Mill) K. Koch

(1) The bark of ironwood and *Magnolia acuminata* are made into a decoction. For toothache, hold the hot decoction in the mouth and spit it out when it has cooled. Repeat as often as needed (W. W.).

^{d_j}u·ti n$\propto$, *(W. W.), "ironwood."*

BEECH FAMILY *Fagaceae*

American Chestnut
Castanea dentata (Marsh) Borkh.

(1) Collect from off the ground year-old chestnut leaves. Boil them for a short time and drink the tea for heart trouble (T. L.). (2) Leaves collected from young sprouts will cure old sores (A. L.). (3) Chestnuts are ground into flour, which is used in making a bread (A. L.). (4) An infusion drunk for the cure of a type of tuberculosis caused by incantation includes the barks of chestnut, *Carya spp., Liriodendron tulipifera,* and *Tilia spp., Fagus grandifolia,* and *Quercus spp.* (W. W.). (5) A steep of the barks of four trees is a good medicine for monthly female trouble: chestnut, *Acer*

rubrum, Quercus alba, and *Q. nigra* (Y. J.). (6) Of the bark is made a rich brown dye (M. A.). (7) Sometimes women, after giving birth to a baby, won't stop bleeding and begin cramping. Prepare a cold infusion of the barks of chestnut and *Aesculus spp.* and give them to drink "...not too much of it, or it will stop everything" (Y. J.). (8) Prepare a decoction of the leaves of chestnut and *Verbascum thapsus* and mix with brown sugar or honey. Use as a cough syrup (M. A.). (9) To make the navel of an infant recede. Collect the small galls of a chestnut tree which are close to the ground, heat in the hearth of a fireplace. Take four of these and allow them to cool to the point where the child can stand the heat. With each of the galls, hit the child's navel for four nights, if necessary, until the navel recedes (N. A.).

Ti li, *(A. L., T. L., N. A.), "chestnut."*

Chinquapin
Castanea pumila (L.) Mill.

(1) Used for fevers. (2) Used in the medicine accompanying Formula 30: "For fever blisters."

U ni gi neg∝at ki, *(Olbrecht, 1932), "chinquapin."*

Beech
Fagus grandifolia Ehrh.

(1) An infusion drunk for the cure of a type of tuberculosis caused by incantation includes the barks of beech, *Fagus grandfolia, Castanea dentata, Quercus spp., Liriodendron tulipifera, Tilia spp.* (W. W.). (2) For "bad disease" drink a tea made by boiling for a short time the barks of beech, *Smilax glauca, Euonymus americanus, Nyssa sylvatica, Liquidambar styraciflua, Vitis aestivalis,* and *Platanus occidentalis* (T. L.).

Ku s∝, *(W. W.), "beech."*

Oak
Quercus spp.

(1) An infusion drunk for the cure of a type of tuberculosis caused by incantation includes the barks of oak, *Castanea dentata, Carya spp., Fagus grandifolia, Liriodendron tulipifera,* and *Tilia spp.* (W. W.). (2) Oak splints are used in basketry.

T∝ta, *(Olbrecht, 1932), "oak."*

White Oak
Quercus alba (L.)

(1) An ingredient in the medicine accompanying Formula 49: "For diarrhea." A tea for bowel troubles (A. L., M. A.). (2) The bark of white oak is soaked in cold water. This tea

White Oak
Quercus alba

when applied will bring relief to gall (sore groin), sore armpits, or chapped area. The bark can be chewed for mouth sores (A. L.). (3) A bark tea is used as an emetic (Witthoft, 1947b). (4) A steep of the barks of four trees is a good medicine for monthly female trouble: white oak, *Quercus nigra, Acer rubrum,* and *Castanea dentata* (Y. J.).

T$^{(}$$\propto$^{d}ta, *(Olbrecht, 1932),* "oak," Ta la, *(Y. J.).*

Spanish Oak
Quercus falcata Michx.

(1) An alternate ingredient in the medicine accompanying Formula 21: "For aggravated hoarseness."

Gu lE^{+}sus ti ga, *(Olbrecht, 1932),* "oak."

Shingle Oak
Quercus imbricaria Michx.

The Cherokee name and usage is the same as *Q. falcata,* above.

Water Oak
Quercus nigra (L.)

(1) A steep of the barks of four trees is a good medicine for monthly female trouble: water oak, *Quercus alba, Castanea dentata, Acer rubrum* (Y. J.).

Gu la nEgwa, *(Y. J.),* "water oak."

Red Oak
Quercus rubra (L.)

(1) An ingredient in the medicine accompanying Formula 49: "For diarrhea."

D ɔ·^{u}l$\propto$$^{+}$si, *(Olbrecht, 1932),* "red oak."

Post Oak
Quercus stellata Wang.

(1) An ingredient in the medicine accompanying Formula 22: "For milky urine."

$^{+}$Su^{i}us ka, *(Olbrecht, 1932),* $^{+}$Sus ka, *(Olbrecht, 1932),* "post oak."

Black Oak
Quercus velutina Lam.

(1) Leaves of this oak and other oaks having large leaves are used to wrap dough for boiling in bread-making (A. L.). (2) A bark tea is drunk for relief of asthma (Lloyd Lambert).

ELM FAMILY *Ulmaceae*

Slippery Elm
Ulmus rubra Muhl.

(1) An ingredient in the medicine accompanying Formula 49: "For diarrhea." (2) A decoction including a cone of *Pinus pungens*, the stem of *Impatiens capensis*, the root of *Veronica officinalis*, and the bark of slippery elm is given to pregnant women before going to the water each new moon. The elm is used because the slippery character of its sap is believed to aid in the delivery of the child (Olbrecht, 1932). (3) Chew inside bark and spit on baseball glove–makes the ball stick to the glove (N. A.). (4) For burns, make a steep of the bark and wash (A. L.). (5) Old people grow the trees for medicine (T. L.).

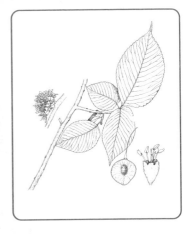

D∝u w^{e}^{dz}i la, *(Olbrecht, 1932),* I·dah∝, *(N. A.),* D∝^{i}wa^{dz}i la, *(Olbrecht, 1932),* Da w∝^{dz}i ła, *(T. L.),* "elm."

NETTLE FAMILY *Urticaceae*

Rich Weed, Toe Itch
Pilea pumila (L) Gray

(1) An infusion is made to reduce the excessive hunger of children (A. L.). (2) Rub the stem between the toes for itching (L. H.).

U ni·ya lu gi ski, *(A. L.).*

Bear Nettle
Urtica gracilis Ait.

(1) Medicine for upset stomach. Burn off the stickers and rub on (T. L.). (2) The leaves, stems and pounded roots are soaked in water and warmed. The tea is drunk for ague (W. W.). (3) The twisted stems are used for bow strings (Y. J.).

TɔlEdɔ́, *(N. A., T. L.),* To lEdɔa ta^{d}sɔsti, *(W. W.), "stinging on you."*

SANDALWOOD FAMILY *Santalaceae*

Bastard Toadflax
Comandra umbellata (L.) Nutt

(1) Pick a leaf and put the juice which oozes out on a cut or sore to make it heal (C. S.) (confusion with Euphorbia?). (2) A hot infusion of bastard toadflax and *Cypripedium spp.* is drunk for kidney trouble (M. S.).

U·na da ta skis ́ kɔ, *(C. S.), "pus it oozes out,"* Ga ni gwa li sgi, *(Olbrecht, 1932, M. S.),* "clotted blood" or "it is bruised."

Oilnut
Pyrularia pubera Michx.

(1) Roast the ripe fruit and pulverize it by rubbing on a rock or some rough object. Use this as a salve for sores (Mandy Walkingstick). Roast and grate the fruits and mix with tallow for old sore salve (A. L.). Make a poultice of the pounded root and bear oil and apply to old sores. "It healed an eighteen year-old sore" (N. C.).

$^+$Si gwa gwa, *(N. C.).*

MISTLETOE FAMILY *Loranthaceae*

Mistletoe
Phoradendron flavescens (Pursh.) Nutt

(1) Mistletoe, found on the ground where it has fallen, steeped in hot water is a medicine

Mistletoe
Phoradendron flavescens

for pregnant women. The tea helps to get the baby from the mother quickly (Olbrecht, 1932). (2) Make a tea ooze and bathe the head with it for a headache (A. L.). (3) To cure lovesickness, vomit for four days, then drink of mistletoe tea (W. W.).

U daɫɔ́, *(N. A.),* Uda⁺ɫi, *(A. L., T. L.),* U dat‛í·, *(W. W.), "married to another kind" (a word expressing an immoral relationship? A. L. would not translate this meaning saying "I don't know what it means.")*

BIRTHWORT FAMILY *Aristolochiaceae*

Dutchman's Pipe
Aristolochia macrophylla Hill

(1) An ingredient used in the medicine accompanying Formula 81: "For urinary trouble."

U·dɔ·i utɛnↄ́, *(Olbrecht, 1932).*

Virginia Snakeroot
Aristolochia serpentaria (L.)

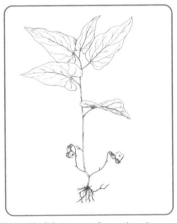

(1) An alternate ingredient used in the medicine accompanying Formula 5: "For when he dreams of snakes." (2) For sharp pains. (3) Used in the medicine accompanying Formula 39: "For dizziness, fainting, or headaches." A cold root tea is drunk to relieve headache (Y. J.). (4) An alternate ingredient in the medicine of Formula 80: "For itching privates when one has urinated on a fire." (5) A root decoction is drunk for stomach ache (A. L.). A cold root tea is drunk for stomach ache (Y. J.). (6) A root decoction is blown on the patient for fever and feverish headaches (Mooney, 1885). A root steep is drunk for fever. A prayer is recited (W. W.). (7) A root decoction is drunk for coughs (Mooney, 1885). (8) To cure snakebite, chew the root and spit upon the wound (Ibid). (9) To relieve a toothache, place a piece of the root in the hollow tooth (Ibid). (10) Boil the root for a short while and drink the tea for heart trouble (T. L.). (11) Drink a root tea or chew the root and swallow the juice for colds (N. A.). A cold root tea (infusion) is good for colds (Y. J.). (12) If a person gets wounded in an accident (cut with an axe, etc.) a cold infusion of the entire plant when drunk will relieve the pain and prevent fainting (Y. J.). (13) The bruised root will bring relief when held against a nose made sore by constant blowing of colds (Mooney, 1885).

Virginia Snakeroot
Aristolochia serpentaria

U nas tE⁺s⁺s yu, *(N. A., Y. J.)*, U n∝stE·⁺si⁺si ga, *(Olbrecht, 1932)*, St∝st ga, *(W. W.)*, *"little root," "root."*

Wild Ginger
Asarum canadense (L.)

(1) An ingredient used in the medicine accompanying Formula 29: "For swollen breast." (2) An ingredient in the medicine accompanying Formula 54: "For abdominal pains caused by the terrapin." (3) The leaves dried and pounded are used for snuff (Witthoft, 1947b). (4) The fresh leaves are applied to wounds (Ibid). (5) A root tea is drunk for colds (N. C.). (6) A decoction of wild ginger, *Goodyera pubescens, Alnus serrulata, Prunus serotina,* and *Xanthorhiza simplicissima* is a good blood tonic. "Take several swallows before a meal... builds the appetite" (M. A.). (7) A root infusion is drunk for monthly period pains (M. A.). A tea for female complaint (A. L.). (8) A root tea is drunk for heart trouble (M. A., T. L.). A beaten root tea is taken for the heart (Lottie May Squirrel).

Lu i ga⁺li, *(W. W.)*, *"climbing,"* Skwɔ·lu· tɔna, *Olbrecht, 1932)*, Nu y∝ga⁺li, *(W. W.)*, Skwa li, *(N. C., N. A.)*, U nis k∝l∝ᵈʲunt∝n∝, *(W. W.)*.

BUCKWHEAT FAMILY *Polygonaceae*

Knotweed
Polygonum aviculare (L.)

(1) A root infusion for a child taking the flux (Y. J.).
(2) A tea is drunk for kidney trouble (A. L.).

Smartweed
Polygonum hydropiper (L.)

(1) The plant was used to poison fish a long time ago—it is no longer used (W. W.). (2) The

Smartweed
Polygonum hydropiper

plant is cooked up and used in a poultice for swollen joints or bruises. The crushed roots, leaves, or flowers are applied to bruises or pains as a liniment. It is strong (C. S.). Wring the plant up, cook it and mix with cornmeal for a poultice to be used for pain (H. R.). (3) Rub the leaves on children's fingers to prevent thumb sucking (Bettie Owle).

Ga ni Kwi li·sti, *(A. L.), "clotted blood," or* "it is bruised," U yↄ∝ns ti, *(C. S.).*

Sheep Sorrel
Rumex acetosella (L.)

(1) The leaves are used as a poultice for sores (A. L.).
ᵈsunↄ ᵈsunↄ ᵈᶻa ⁱsti, *(A. L.), "sour."*

Yellow Dock
Rumex crispus (L.)

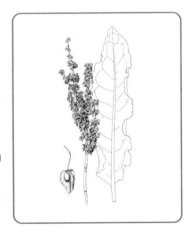

(1) Beat up the roots and feed them to a horse when it is sick to its stomach (A. L.). (2) A root tea is given to a woman in childbirth labor (A. L.). (3) A root tea is good for the blood. "My mother has used it in the spring when every scratch will cause a sore and sickness" (M. A.). (4) A root tea will break up constipation (Sam Owle). (5) In late pregnancy (the last five months) boil a big piece of the root in a gallon of water—boil down to three quarts. This tea, when drunk, will keep down the blood loss in childbirth (N. A.).

ᵗsↄKwↄli di ka nↄ∝wↄ, *(A. L.), "sour."*

Jumpseed
Polygonum virginianum (L.) Raf.

(1) A hot tea of the leaves of jumpseed and the bark of *Gleditsia triacanthos* is given to those with whooping cough (N. A.).

Daↄni yuh sti, *(A. L.),* A⁺sEhi, *(N. A.).*

45

GOOSEFOOT FAMILY *Chenopodiaceae*

Jerusalem Oak, Vermifuge
Chenopodium ambrosioides (L.)

(1) Boil a stem and leaf decoction to a thick consistency, cool, and cut into bite-size blocks. Give these to children to rid them of hookworms. No water must be drunk during the treatment (T. L., A. L.). Beat up the tops and roots and make a tea by pouring over it hot water. Take no breakfast and drink the tea from early morning to noon to get rid of worms (Mooney, Ms.). Make a thick syrup of the seeds and add molasses. Take the mixture for worms (H. R., M. A., Minnie Saunooke). (2) A warm root tea is drunk in the winter for "fever disease" (Y. L.). (3) For colds and headache make a cold tea; drink and moisten the head with it (N. A.).

Dilɑgows'ɑgí, *(T. L.),* Di ga ya su gí gows'ɑgí wa ti gÉ, *(A. L.),* "it smells," U ni^tsi yú su hi yu stí, *(Mooney, Ms.),* Di lá, *(N. A.).*

AMARANTH FAMILY *Amaranthaceae*

Green Amaranth
Amaranthus retroflexus (L.)

(1) An alternate ingredient in a green corn medicine (see Appendix).
Wats'ká, *(W. W.).*

Spring Amaranth
Amaranthus spinosus (L.)

(1) An alternate ingredient in a green corn medicine (see Appendix).
To lEti yu stí, *(W. W.),* "stick on you, like."

FOUR-O'CLOCK FAMILY *Nyctaginaceae*

Four-o'clock
Mirabilis spp.

(1) Milk which has been poured over the leaves of four-o'clock is a fly poison (H. R.).

POKEWEED FAMILY *Phytolaccaceae*

Poke
Phytolacca americana (L.)

(1) The leaves are eaten in salads in early spring (T. L., N. A., N. C., W. W.). "In the spring

Poke
Phytolacca americana

of the year, bear-bacon is a favorite dish with the traders, along with herbs that the woods afford in plenty...especially with the young tops of poke, the root of which is a very strong poison. And this method they pursue year by year, as a physical regimen, in order to purge their blood" (Adair, 1775). (2) Beat the dried roots fine and sprinkle the powder on old sores (N. A.). (3) The roots are boiled and the tea is used for eczema. The tea is either applied or put in the bath water. The tea is also effective in curing chickens of "cholera" (appearing to the writer to be a deficiency disease in undernourished fowl) (H. R.). (4) Beat the root fine and put in cold water. This tea will cause the urine to flow more easily (T. L.). (5) Poke berry wine will relieve rheumatism. Add sugar to the crushed fruit and allow to ferment. The wine is taken a tablespoon at a time (A. L., M. A.). The berries, when eaten, will relieve rheumatism (H. R., L. H.). (6) The crushed berries add color to canned fruit (T. L.). (7) Poke greens are good for building up the blood (M. A.).

^{dz}ay it agᴏᴄ, *(W. W.),* ^{dz}a ˡdᴏᴄgáᴏᴄ, *(A. L.), (N. A.), "poke."*

PINK FAMILY *Caryophyllaceae*

Common Chickweed
Cerastium vulgatum (L.)

(1) A decoction of the stem of chickweed and the root of *Cypripedium calceolus var. parviflorum* is used for worms in children (Mooney, 1885).

BUTTERCUP FAMILY *Ranunculaceae*

Doll's Eyes
Actaea alba Eli

(1) An ingredient in the medicine accompanying Formula 75: "For chills." (2) This will kill the teeth of young people if they are not careful with it (Y. J.). (3) This is used for swelling of the leg which is caused by the biting of spirit insects which are in the flesh. Boil the root, make a really hot tea, and bathe the foot in it. Bathe and wash the leg until the brew cools. This will drive the spirit insects from the flesh (W. W.).

U li das ti us ti ga, *(Olbrecht, 1932), "he deceives, it is little,"* Ka nos ta gwa ɫi, *(N. A.),* Kᴏᴄno·stᴏᴄgwa li, *(W. W.).*

Wood Anemone
Anemone quinquefolia (L.)

(1) This is used in an attraction medicine (love formula). Get the root before the spring winds blow, it is no good after that; it has a long root. Hold the root in the hands and rub between them while reciting the formula (W. W.).

Yɔn wi^{dj}un sti´ u wa^{+}za lɔ, *(W. W.), "little people's saliva."*

Thimbleweed
Anemone virginiana (L.)

(1) A root tea is is used to cure the whooping cough (N. C.).

$^{dz.}$i stu´ us ka lɔn ti, *(A. L.), "rabbit."*

Columbine
Aquilegia canadensis (L.)

(1) A cold infusion will stop the flux (Y. J.).

Gigɔgɛa^{dz}ilɔski´, *(Y. J.), "blood-like, it is a flower,"* La lu´ni, *(C. S.),*

Black Snakeroot
Cimicifuga racemosa (L.) Nutt.

(1) The roots in alcoholic spirits were used to relieve rheumatic pains (Witthoft, 1947b). (2) An ingredient in the medicine accompanying Formula 75: "For chills."

U li dɔsti´ utɔnoɔ, *(Olbrecht, 1932),* "he deceives, it is tall."

Virgin's Bower
Clematis virginiana (L.)

(1) An ingredient in the medicine accompanying Formula 81: "For urinary trouble." "Sunlight," with other ingredients, is steeped and drunk as a medicine for yellow, painful urination (W. W.). A root tea is drunk by children or adults for kidney trouble. "When the water won't stop" (Nephritis?) (Y. J., A. L.). Boil the roots for one hour, reducing a gallon of water to a three-quart decoction. Drink all you can before retiring; during the night you wake up in a deep sweat. This is a good medicine for the bladder and kidneys (N. A.). (2) This is one of the ingredients in a medicine to be drunk if you get sick eating the first harvest of roasting ears (N. C.). (3) A warm infusion of "sunlight" and *Asclepias*

Virgin's Bower
Clematis virginiana

perennis is drunk for backache, or the roots may be chewed instead. Salt is forbidden (T. L.). (4) A root infusion is drunk for stomach trouble (ulcers, etc.) (A. L.).

U·dɑ·i us ti ga, *(Olbrecht, 1932), "little vine,"* I ga ga ti, *(W. W., T. L., N. A.),* E ga·gɑti, *(A. L.), "sunlight,"* O si wɑni, *(N. C.), "grows on the hot house."*

Larkspur
Delphinium spp.

(1) Root makes cow drunk and kills him (M. S.).

Wa ga ᵈⁱu ni hi hi, *(M. S.), "cattle not supposed to eat."*

Round-lobed Hepatica
Hepatica americana (D. C.) Key

(1) An ingredient in the medicine accompanying Formula 29: "For swollen breasts." (2) An ingredient in the medicine accompanying Formula 54: "For abdominal pains caused by the terrapin." (3) Used for coughs either in tea or by chewing roots (Mooney, 1885). (4) "...Those who dream of snakes drink a decoction of this herb and ...*Camptosorus rhizophyllus* to produce vomiting, after which the dreams do not return. The traders buy large quantities of liverwort from the Cherokees, who may have learned to esteem it more highly than they otherwise would" (Mooney, 1885). (5) Hot root tea is drunk for bowel trouble (A. L.). (6) Boil the root, give the tea to children to drink every moon to keep off epidemics like whooping cough, measles, etc. (W. W.). (7) Smoke the dried, crumpled leaves for heart trouble (T. L.). (8) For toothache in the spring, beat up the leaves and make a tea. Hold the tea in the mouth (N. A.).

Skwɔ·lu sti ga, *(Olbrecht, 1932),* Skwa li, *(A. L., N. A.),* Uni·skwa·li, *(W. W.), "hepatica."*

Hepatica
Hepatica acutiloba (D. C.)

The usages are similar to *Hepatica americana.*

Uni skwɔli^{′dj}un stí, *(T. L.), "hepatica, little."*

Early Meadow-rue
Thalictrum dioicum (L.)

(1) A root tea is prepared for diarrhea (A. L.). A decoction of the root is drunk for diarrhea with vomiting (Mooney, 1885).

A⁺za tí wa^{dz.}is ká, *(W. W., A. L.), "fish scales."*

Globe Flower
Trollius laxus Salisb.

(1) The leaves and stem are steeped in boiling water for "thrash" (M. S.). *(Introduced)*

Yellow Root
Xanthoriza simplicissima Marsh.

(1) Used in the medicine accompanying Formula 70: "For childbirth." (2) Bathe the eyes with a bark ooze to relieve them of soreness (A. L.). For sore eyes, make a poultice by wrapping scraped bark in flannel and moistening until wet (N. A.). (3) For sore mouth, chew the root or use an infusion as a mouth wash (N. C., M. A., Lottie May Squirrel, Sam Owle). (4) Yellow root is an ingredient which is mixed in mutton tallow for a salve for sores (M. A.). (5) A root tea is drunk for cramps (Amonite Sequoyah). (6) The root is used as a dye material (Leftwich, 1952). (7) A decoction of yellow root, *Asarum canadense, Goodyera pubescens, Alnus serrulata,* and *Prunus serotina* is a good blood tonic. "Take several swallows before a meal...builds the appetite" (M. A.). (8) A tea for nerves (H. R.).

Di lɔ·ní, *(Y. J.), "yellow,"* Dɔlɔni unɔstE^{dz}í, *(W. W.), "yellow root."*

BARBERRY FAMILY *Berberidaceae*

Blue Cohosh
Caulophyllum thalictroides (L.) Pers.

(1) For toothache, hold the root tea ooze in the mouth (A. L.). When teeth are rotting, chew the root or drink tea. The teeth will be poisoned in three or four years (M. A.). Rub leaves on "oak poison"–kills it right away (C. S.). (3) Root tea for after pains (M. A.).

Blue Cohosh
Caulophyllum thalictroides

U·lì das di, *(A. L., C. S.), "he deceives,"*
Ka nɔstɔɡwa li, *(?).*

May-apple
Podophyllum peltatum (L.)

(1) Indians used to sell the root a long time ago, but no medicine of it is known (T. L.). (Olbrecht, 1932, felt that the white traders may have caused importance to be laid on collected herbs). (2) Beat up the roots and make an ooze of them. Soak corn in this ooze before planting to keep off crows (A. L.). Soak corn in root tea ooze as an insect repellant (H. R.). The joints of the roots are a poison. Cut out the parts between the joints, mash, and boil for medicine (C. S.). (3) Beat up the roots fine like a meal. A teaspoonful of this powder is used as a laxative (N. A.). Bake the root in

an oven or in the sun until dry. A small piece of the internode of the root taken as a pill will "clean you out" (A. L.). A root tea for bowels (Amonite Sequoyah). A syrup is boiled of the root and given for a purgative, two pills at a time (Witthoft, 1947b). (4) A drop of the juice of the fresh root in the ear is a cure for deafness (So I have been told, I never witnessed it (Witthoft, 1947b). (5) The root soaked in whiskey is drunk for rheumatism (A. L.).

U nEskwEtu gɔ, *(A. L., J. L.)*, U ni skwEtugɔ, *(C. S.)*, Una gui sti, *(N. A.)*,
U wil shwEtu gi, *(C. S.)*.

MAGNOLIA FAMILY *Magnoliaceae*

Tuliptree, Yellow Poplar
Liriodendron tulipifera (L.)

(1) An alternate ingredient in the medicine accompanying Formula 5: "For when he dreams of snakes." (2) An alternate ingredient in the medicine accompanying Formula 80: "For itching privates when one has urinated in the fire." (3) An ingredient in the medicine

Tuliptree, Yellow Poplar
Liriodendron tulipifera

accompanying Formula 86: "For indigestion." (4) In ancient times a log of poplar was used in making a dugout canoe. The Cherokee name for "poplar" also means "canoe" (John Witthoft). (5) A decoction of the bark of poplar is blown with a tube on fractured limbs to help them heal. The arm is splinted and rest is prescribed (Olbrecht, 1932). (6) For indigestion, drink an infusion made by steeping the root or root bark (pounded) of a young tree about two feet in height (W. W.). (7) A bark tea for stomach trouble (H. R.). (8) A decoction of the root bark is made and given in fevers (Olbrecht, 1932). (9) A bark decoction is drunk for bowel trouble (Peter Long). (10) The bark is used as a preservative in home-made medicine (T. L.). (11) Skin off some of the bark and dry it in an oven. Powder the bark and take a small quantity (on the end of a knife) for pinworms (H. R.). (12) Infusion drunk for the cure of a type of tuberculosis caused by incantation includes the barks of poplar, *Quercus spp.*, *Carya spp.*, *Castanea dentata*, *Fagus grandifolia*, and *Tilia spp.* (W. W.).

^dGi yúh, *(T. L., A. L., Y. J., W. W.),* ⁺Si gú, *(Olbrecht, 1932) "poplar."*

Cucumber Tree
Magnolia acuminata (L.)

(1) An ingredient in the medicine accompanying Formula 86: "For indigestion." (2) The barks of "big leaves" and *Ostrya virginiana* are make into a decoction. For toothache, hold the hot decoction in the mouth and spit it out when it has cooled. Repeat as often as needed (W. W.). (3) A tea of the bark is drunk to relieve cramps in a baby's stomach (in summer) (A. L.). A cold or warm tea is drunk for belching or stomachache (N. A.). (4) The bark of a cucumber tree is one ingredient in a medicine for "bloody flux" (A. L.).

^{dj}u yᴐsti, *(N. A.),* ⁺Su yᴐsti, *(Olbrecht, 1932),* "they are bitter," ⁺Su glo·^{dj}E·gwa, *(W. W.),* "big leaves."

CALYCANTHUS FAMILY *Calycanthaceae*

All Spice
Calycanthus fertilis Walt

(1) An ingredient in the medicine accompanying Formula 55: "For irregular urination."

All Spice
Calycanthus fertilis

(2) For a person who is losing his eyesight, drip a cold bark tea into the eyes from a saturated rag. "...will take white stuff off the eyeball" (N. A.). (3) A bark ooze will cure children's sores (A. L.). Bark tea for a baby's hives (M. A.).

KⵆnE·tska, *(Olbrecht, 1932, T. L.),* Ka nEs⁽í⁾
(N. A.).

Strawberry Shrub
Calycanthus floridus (L.)

(1) The roots are used (though very strong) in an emetic. The seeds poison wolves (Witthoft, 1947b).

CUSTARD–APPLE FAMILY *Annonaceae*

Paw Paw
Asimina triloba (L.) Dunal

(1) Of the bark they made very strong ropes (Witthoft, 1947b). The bark is twisted into a string (Bascom Walkingstick).

Deshⵆg⁽í⁾, *(T. L., Bascom Walkingstick), "paw paw."*

LAUREL FAMILY *Lauraceae*

Blume, Spicebush
Lindera benzoin (L.)

(1) A bunch of twigs as big as your fist is boiled in water for a short time for a beverage tea (A. L., N. A., L. H.). (2) The barks of spicebush, *Cornus florida,* and *Prunus serotina* are steeped. Add this tea to pure corn whiskey and drink to break out the measles (A. L.). (3) Boil together the bark of spicebush and *Hamamelis virginiana,* and some needles of *Pinus virginiana* for five or 10 minutes. To "break out" fever, drink this tea hot and cover up (T. L.). (4) Give tea to a baby to drink for hives (H. R.). (5) Drink cool, sweet tea for red measles (Bettie Owle).

Nɔ?da⁺li, *(A. L.),* No?stⵆᵈgí, *(N. A.),* Nɔ·ta⁺sí, *(T. L.), "spicebush."*

Sassafras
Sassafras albidum (Nutt.) Ness.

(1) Steep the bark of the tap root in hot water and drink for diarrhea or flux (W. W.). Drink the root tea daily for bowels (Kimsey Squirrel). (2) The root tea is drunk as a blood builder (H. R., M. A., T. L., A. L.). The root of sassafras (or the gum of *Pinus virginiana*) was used in the old days to flavor homemade soap (see *P. virginiana*) (A. L.). (4) A root poultice is applied to sores anywhere on the body: sprained ankles, bruises, etc. (N. A.). (5) For sore eyes (styes, pink eye, etc.) make a cold eyewash of the pith. "My mother used it all the time" (M. A.). (6) A root tea is drunk for headaches and colds (N. A.). (7) A few pieces of the bark or root are boiled for a short time in water for a beverage tea (N. A., L. H.).

Gan sta^{dz}a, *(Kimsey Squirrel),* Kan·?sta$^+$chi, *(W. W.),* Kan sta^{dz}i, *(A. L., N. A.),* "sassafras."

POPPY FAMILY *Papaveraceae*

Bloodroot
Sanguinaria canadensis (L.)

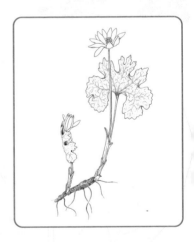

(1) The red juice of the root is used in basketry dye (Speck, 1920 A. L., N. A., Witthoft, 1947b). (2) Soak the root in cold water and drink for cough medicine (T. L.). (3) Dry the root, pulverize, and sniff the powder for catarrh (A. L.).

Gi gɔgÉunaS tE^{dz}i, *(W. W.),* "red root," Gi tɬi wa$^(i$tɔ, *(A. L.),* "dog penis."

MUSTARD FAMILY *Brassicaceae*

Shepherd's Purse
Capsella bursa-pastoris (L.) Medic.

(1) In early spring the young leaves are often eaten for salad, raw or with salt (N. A.). The spring greens are cooked (W. W.).

U lis$^(i$i, *(N. A.),* U lis$^(i$i utɔnaɔ, *(W. W.).*

Toothwort
Cardamine diphylla Michx.

(1) Beat up the roots and put in a poultice for headache (T. L.).

A nⱭskwⱭlⱭski, *(T. L.).*

Crow's Foot, Toothwort
Cardamine heterophylla Nutt.

(1) A poultice of the beaten-up roots draws out the
pain of headaches, etc. Apply for a full day or two
full days (N. A., Y. J.). (2) The greens are eaten in
early spring (Y. J.). This toothwort is an ingredient
in a salad "to fill belly" made with grease and onions
(N. C.). (3) Some people chew the root (it is strong) for
colds (Y. J.). (4) A tea of the roots is drunk for sore
throat (Y. J.).

A na skwⱭlas gi, A na li skwa la gi ski,
Nɔsqui len ski, *(N. C.).*

Watercress
Rorippa nasturtium-aquaticum R. Br.

(1) The greens are eaten in salads (N. A.).

A mayi u du hi u di gⱭnEhi, *(N. A.).*

Hedge Mustard
Sisymbrium officinale (L.) Scop.

(1) It grows wild in yards. An old field weed used in salads (N. A.).

E gwa u lis i, *(N. A.), "grandchild."*

PITCHER PLANT FAMILY *Sarraceniaceae*

Pitcher Plant
Sarracenia purpurea (L.)

(The writer could find no informant who could recognize a mounted specimen, yet
Olbrecht reported its use with Cherokee names.) (1) Drink the water found in this flower to
obtain a never failing memory—for medicine man initiates (Olbrecht, 1932).

Yu gwi la, *(Olbrecht, 1932),* Yu gwe li, *(M. O.),* Yu gwi lu, *(W. W.).*

SAXIFRAGE FAMILY *Saxifragaceae*

Alum Root
Heuchera americana (L.)

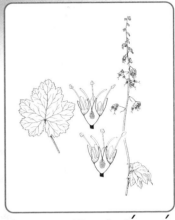

(1) Chew the root to take the coat off the tongue (T. L.).
(2) Drink root tea for grumbling stomach (dysentery),
a cupful at night (A. L.). Drink for dysentery. (3) For
"thrash," make a cold tea of the finely beaten roots.
Allow the powder to sit in the cold water for several
hours (Y. J.). (4) For bad sores during the "dog days"
of late summer, make a tea (warm or cold) and sprinkle
on. The scab will fall off and new skin will form
underneath (N. A.).

A dan?gu la gi skí U nɛgɔ̃, *(T. L.), "coated tongue, white,"* Uɔy da lí us tí,
"sweet flag, little," ⁺Su ha lɔ̃ga·'É, *(A. L.),* da yɛkwá, *(N. A.).*

Wild Hydrangea, Seven Bark
Hydrangea arborescens (L.)

(1) An ingredient in the medicine accompanying
Formula 15: "For disordered bile." (2) An
ingredient in the medicine accompanying Formula 51:
"For menstruating women who dream of giving birth
to animals or unnatural beings." (3) To stop vomiting
in children from 18 months to 10 years, make a cold
tea of the inner bark. Collect when green (N. A., A. L.,
T. L., Y. J., M. A.). (4) Bind on freshly scraped bark for
burns or risings (H. R.). (5) A poultice is made for sore
or swollen muscles (C. S.).

Di dɔ̃nɛlɔ̃wɔ·skí, *(Olbrecht, 1932, N. A.),*
Di dɔ̃nɛgɔ̃lis kí, *(A. L.), "peal off,"* Su lu yi ł gá, *(Olbrecht, 1932), "swamp
tree,"* U tahí, *(T. L.).*

Swamp Saxifrage
Saxifraga pensylvanica (L.)

(1) The leaves are eaten green (as lettuce) in salads (N. C.). (2) A root poultice is made for
sore and swollen muscles (C. S.).
ᵈᶻo·li yu stí, *(C. S.). "tobacco-like,"* A wi gangɔ̃, *(N. C.).*

Swamp Saxifrage
Saxifraga pennsylvanica

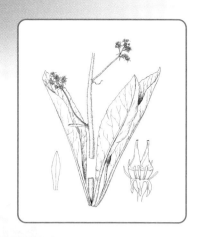

Foamflower
Tiarella spp.

(1) A tea is held in the mouth to remove the white coat from the tongue (T. L.).

Ad⸲?ga la gi skí unEgᴂ, *(T. L.).*

WITCH HAZEL FAMILY *Hamamelidaceae*

Witch Hazel
Hamamelis virginiana (L.)

(1) A bark decoction will relieve a sore throat (Minnie Saunooke). (2) Pour hot water over the bark to make a tea for colds (A. L.). (3) The bark of witch hazel and *Lindera benzoin,* and the needles of *Pinus virginiana* are made into a hot decoction (boiling five or 10 minutes). The patient drinks the tea, covers up, and his fever "breaks out" (T. L.).

Ka na su dà sᴂwá, *(T. L.), "witch hazel."*

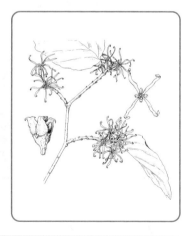

Sweetgum
Liquidambar styraciflua (L.)

(1) Boil for a short time the barks of sweetgum, *Euonymus americanus, Vitis aestivalis, Platanus occidentalis, Fagus grandiflora, Smilax glauca,* and *Nyssa sylvatica* — a tea for "bad disease" (T. L.). (2) Knock off a piece of the bark and return in a week to collect the hardened sap for chewing gum (N. A., L. H.). (3) Of the inner bark a tea is made for nervous patients (Witthoft, 1947b). (4) The gum is used for drawing plaster (Witthoft, 1947b).

Sweetgum

Liquidambar styraciflua

^dJi la li´, *(T. L.),* ^dJi·yɔli´, *(N. A.),* ^dZi lɔlu´, *(A. L.),* *"sweetgum."*

SYCAMORE FAMILY *Plantanaceae*

Sycamore
Platanus occidentalis (L.)

(1) An ingredient in the medicine accompanying Formula 22: "For milky urine." (2) An ingredient in the Formula 49: "For diarrhea or dysentery." (3) An ingredient in the medicine accompanying Formula 51: "For menstruating women who dream of giving birth to animals or unnatural beings." (4) An ingredient in the medicine accompanying Formula 76: "For afterbirth." A decoction of the roots of sycamore, *Tsuga caroliniana,* and *Smilax glauca* is drunk for afterbirth (Olbrecht, 1932). (5) Boil for a short time the barks of sycamore, *Liquidambar styraciflua, Euonymus americanus, Vitis aestivalis, Fagus grandifolia, Smilax glauca,* and *Nyssa sylvatica* – a tea for bad disease (T. L.). (6) When a sore becomes infected, wash it off with a bark ooze of sycamore (A. L.). (7) Beat the bark fine and make a tea for infants. When their faces break out and peel, wash with this tea and new skin will grow back like the young sprouts of a sycamore (N. A.).

Ku wa´ unE·ga´, *(Olbrecht, 1932),* *"mulberry, big,"* Ku wi´ yus ti´, *(T. L.),* Ku wi´ yus ti unE´?, *(A. L.),* *"like mulberry."*

ROSE FAMILY *Rosaceae*

Agrimony
Agrimonia parviflora Ait.

(1) Used in the medicine accompanying Formula 71: "For bowel trouble." Beat up the root

Agrimony
Agrimonia parviflora

balls, put in cold water, and drink for bowels (L. H.). (2)
When I was a girl and the children couldn't get enough
food to fill them up, my mother gave them the root tea
of this to satisfy their hunger (A. L.).

U ni ga nasⱥhá́ nⱥwa ti alⱥsta tí, *(A. L.),*
Kⱥn^dj i stu gá́ u nit ɫigⱥ⁺lⱥdoÉ́,
(Olbrecht, 1932).

Serviceberry
Amelanchier canadensis (L.) Medic.

(1) An ingredient in the medicine accompanying
Formula 78: "For bad diarrhea" (also W. W. and A. L.).
(2) The berries are canned for winter use (N. A.).
Udɔ·lⱥnɔ́, *(W. W.),* Udɔlⱥnɔ́, *(A. L.),*
Udɔ·li ní, *(T. L., N. A.),* "*serviceberry.*"

Goat's Beard
Aruncus dioicus (Walt.) Fern.

(1) Beat the root fine and boil for a while in water.
Allow the tea to cool and drink while warm to stop
excessive urination (Y. J.). (2) For bee stings in the
face or eye, beat the root and apply (A. L.). (3) If the
feet are swollen, make a root "ooze" (infusion) and
bathe the feet (A. L.). (4) A hot root tea given to
pregnant women will keep them from losing too much
blood in childbirth. It will also relieve suffering (N. A.).

Ti li yu sti, *(A. L., Y. J., T. L., M. A.),*
"*chestnut-like.*"

Hawthorn
Crataegus spp.

(1) Bark tea is drunk to give good circulation (A. L.). (2) Bark tea of hawthorn or *Gleditsia triacanthos* is drunk or bathed in by ballplayers to ward off tacklers. "No one wants to run into the thorns" (which these plants have).

T Eli ni, *(A. L.)*, TE·lɔcnɔc, *(T. L., N. A.), "hawthorn."*

American Ipecac, Indian Physic
Porteranthus stipulata (Muhl.) Baill.

(1) The roots of ipecac and *P. trifoliatus* (or the whole plant) are made into a decoction. A pint of this is drunk when an emetic is needed (Witthoft, 1947b).

Indian Physic, Bowman's Root
Porteranthus trifoliatus (L.) Muench

(1) Used in the medicine accompanying Formula 25 and 31: "For soreness in the muscles." (2) This is a bad medicine. The steeped root, if drunk by a woman will make her permanently sterile. "Alright to give to a woman if she cannot bear children and her life depends on it" (W. W.). (3) Boil the root and drink the tea for bowel complaint accompanying fever and vomiting of yellow substance (Mooney, Ms.). Two doctors state that it is good as a tea for bowel complaints, with fever and yellow vomiting, but another says that it is poisonous and that no decoction is ever drunk, but that the beaten root is a good poultice for swelling (Mooney, 1885).
(4) A cold root infusion will relieve bee stings (A. L.). This is good for bee as well as other stings. Make a tea if you have time, or chew the root and apply the juice to the wound (Y. J.). (5) The roots of Bowman's root and *P. stipulata* (or the whole plant) are made into a decoction. A pint of this is drunk when an emetic is needed (Witthoft, 1947b). (6) The pounded root is a good toothache medicine (N. C., N. A.).

A lEu ki ɬ sti, *(A. L.)*, U lɔcu ki lɬɔsti, *(N. C.)*, U lEu stiɔc, *(N. A.), "locust are in a tree, the locust frequents it."* Ti li yu sti, *(W. W.), "chestnut-like."*

Cinquefoil
Potentilla spp.

(1) A mouthwash tea of the finely beaten roots to cure the "thrash" (H. R.). (2) A tea of it is given in fevers (Witthoft, 1947b). (3) In old times the ballplayers ate the root or bathed in a root tea to prevent injury (A. L.). (4) The night before the game the ballplayer would chew the root for wind (N. A.).

A ni yuh sti, *(A. L., N. A.), "strawberry-like."*

Fire Cherry
Prunus pennsylvanica (L.)

(1) An ingredient in the medicine accompanying Formula 72: "For flux." (2) A menstruating woman is forbidden to eat meat of any animal that is shot or it will make her sick. At the beginning of her period, on the first morning, she should drink a warm steep of this bark so that she can eat such meat (W. W.).

Ta yᴂga dᴂsiE hí, *(W. W.), "cherry lives on the mountains,"* Kwᴂn'un sti'gá, *(Olbrecht, 1932), "peaches, very little."*

Peach
Prunus persica (L.) Sieb. & Zuec.

(1) A bark steep is drunk for cough medicine (A. L.). (2) Soak the bark in cold water; use this tea to stop vomiting (M. A.). (M. A. stipulated that in collecting the bark for this medicine the knife must cut upward. For medicines used in treating the bowels, the bark must be cut off in a downward motion. This is suggestive of ancient Indian practice, but no other informant mentioned it). (3) A tea of the bark and cold water is drunk for a sick stomach (H. R.). (4) Cold bark tea and soda is applied to piles (L. H.).

Kwa na, *(A. L.), "peach." (Introduced)*

Black Cherry
Prunus serotina Ehrh.

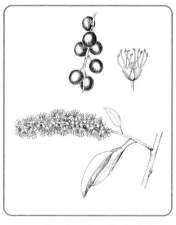

(1) An inner bark decoction is drunk for fever (T. L., Witthoft, 1947b, Y. J.). A decoction of the barks of wild cherry and *Clethra acuminata* is drunk to break a high fever (A. L.). (2) The wood is used for carving (Leftwich, 1952). (3) Boil together the barks of wild cherry, *Lindera benzoin,* and *Cornus florida.* This tea, added to pure corn whiskey, is drunk to break out the measles (A. L.). (4) A bark tea will break up colds (H. R.). (5) A thick bark decoction is taken for coughs (M. A.). (6) A bark infusion is drunk by women just before delivery at the first pangs of childbirth (Olbrecht, 1932). (7) A decoction of wild cherry, *Alnus serrulata, Goodyera pubescens, Asarum canadense,* and *Xanthorhiza simplicissima*

Black Cherry
Prunus serotina

is a good blood tonic. "Take several swallows before a meal...builds up the appetite" (M. A.).

Ta·yáᵅ, *(A. L., T. L., N. A.), "cherry,"* Ta yᵅElu hi, *(W. W), "cherry lowland,"*
Tᵅya inᵅgEhEi i, *(Olbrecht, 1932), "cherry lives on mountains."*

Choke Cherry
Prunus virginiana (L.)

(1) An ingredient in the medicine accompanying
Formula 48: "For fever." (2) An ingredient in the
medicine accompanying Formula 86: "For indigestion."
(3) An ingredient in the medicine accompanying
Formula 21: "For hoarseness."

Tᵅ·ya, *(Olbrecht, 1932), "cherry." (This species
reported by Olbrecht)*

Apple
Pyrus malus (L.)

(1) Used in the medicine accompanying Formula 21:
"For aggravated hoarseness." (2) The bark is used in a
yellow fabric dye (Leftwich, 1952). (3) Mix the bark of
an apple with the "bark" of a two-year-old corn stalk
and make a cold steep. To be drunk by the ballplayers
for dry throat (Source forgotten). (4) In a bucket of
apple juice is put the stem of *Vicia caroliniana* and the
needles of *Pinus virginiana,* which is drunk by the ballplayers for wind during the game (N. A.).

Sunk tá, *"apple,"* Sonk tá a nE yᵓstiᵅghᵓ?
tᵅzu a ti, *"apple." (Introduced)*

Wild Rose
Rosa virginiana Mill.

(1) "If you chew the leaves, they stick in mouth and throat and choke you. Use bark from
stem in medicine without other ingredients" (W. W.). (2) The roots are boiled and the tea is
drunk for dysentery (Witthoft, 1947b).

A da yᵅka li·ski, *(W. W.), "to choke us."*

Southern Blackberry
Rubus argutus

(1) A root tea for bowel complaint (A. L.).

Nu ga ła ga dù aE hi, *(A. L.), "blackberry mountain."*

Blackberry
Rubus flagellaris Willd.

(1) An ingredient in the medicine accompanying
Formula 55: "For irregular urination." (2) Wash the
root, chew it to take the coat off the tongue (T. L.).
(3) Root tea is drunk for summer complaint (H. R.).
Root tea for dysentery (M. A.). (4) The root is good
chew for cough (Witthoft, 1947b).

Nu·ga⁺łɔ, *(Olbrecht, 1932),* Nu ga ła, *(A. L.),*
"blackberry."

Raspberry
Rubus idaeus (L.)

(1) An ingredient in the medicine accompanying Formula 51: "For menstruating women
who dream of giving birth to animals or unnatural beings." (2) If two sisters have babies
and one of the sisters dies, the other sister can nurse the dead sister's baby only if the baby
takes a medicine before suckling. Otherwise, it will sicken and die. Steep the root of regular
wild raspberry growing toward the East and have the baby drink before suckling (W. W.).

Sɔn di wa⁺łi, *(W. W.),* Sö ti wu (d)łi, *(Olbrecht, 1932), "raspberry."*

Black Raspberry
Rubus occidentalis (L.)

(1) An ingredient in the medicine accompanying
Formula 51: "For menstruating women who dream of
giving birth to animals or unnatural beings." (2) The
roots are used for toothache (it is bitter) (T. L.). (3)
"There used to be an old man who made medicines for
use in the ballgame. We would chew on the root of this
and never miss a tackle because of the briers on the
stem" (N. A.). (4) This and other vines with briers are
used for surgical scratching (Olbrecht, 1932).

So ti wu ᵈli, *(Olbrecht, 1932), "raspberry,"*
Nu ga tłɔ, *(T. L.), "blackberry."*

Dewberry
Rubus trivialis Michx.

(1) The roots of dewberry, *Pinus virginiana,* and *Alnus serrulata* (a handful of each) are made into a tea which is good for piles. The tea is drunk and used as a bath (A. L.). *(Identification uncertain, on basis of common name.)*

LEGUME FAMILY *Fabaceae*

Hog Peanut
Amphicarpaea bracteata (L.) Fern.

(1) For snakebite, brew the root and blow the tea on the wound with a prayer and a song. Chewing tobacco can be used as a substitute (W. W.). (2) The herb has a round, edible root (W. W.). (3) A root tea is drunk for diarrhea (A. L.).

Tu ya yu sti, *(T. L.), "bean-like,"* A ni sti, *(W. W.), "threads."*

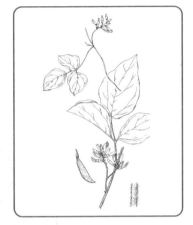

Wild Indigo, Rattlesnake Weed
Baptisia tinctoria (L.) R. Br.

(1) The root is washed, beaten, and put in a hollow tooth for toothache (A. L., Y. J., Lottie May Squirrel). Hold a root tea against the tooth. "It will decay the tooth to the root...you'll never have a toothache in the same tooth" (N. A.). (2) The roots afford a blue dye for fabrics (Leftwich, 1952). (3) A cold tea will stop vomiting (Lloyd Lambert).

A li wᵓtᴐhEski, *(A. L., T. L.),* Dj ni li wᵓtEhE ski, *(W. W.),* Gᶏ li w*ω*ta hE ski, *(Y. J.),* Di·yᴐc shᵓdᵓu di ski, *(N. A.), "leaves moving in every direction," "waving in the wind."*

Partridge-pea
Chamaecrista fasciculata Michx.

(1) A medicine of the roots is given to the ballplayers to keep them from getting tired (T. L.). (2) A tea of partridge-pea and *C. marilandica* is taken for fainting spells (A. L.). (3) "The name and behavior of this plant is sexually symbolic. It is forbidden for man to handle the plant, as it is forbidden for him to handle his penis—if he does, his penis will

Partridge-pea
Cassia fasciculata

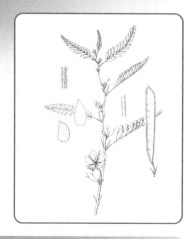

die. A woman can gather this plant and prepare it for medicine. Rub the scraped root on a woman's vulva, makes a man's penis go right in without difficulty; for man who is old or impotent and unable to enter" (M. S.–copied from the field notes of John Witthoft with minor editions to improve continuity).

Ga nɔgi dɔ́, *(M. S.), "has been taken out."*

Wild Sensitive Plant
Chamaecrista nictitans (L.)

(1) The writer believes that the names and usages assigned to *C. fasciculata* are also applicable to wild sensitive plant.

U na̩ gEi⁺sa ga yɔ·Ehi, *(W. W.), "black, grow in old fields."*

Wild Senna
Senna marilandica (L.)

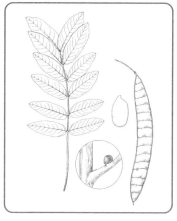

(1) Used for a disease called "black," when a person becomes black around the mouth and eyes—a deadly disease (Cerebral hemorrhage?). Also used for heart trouble. The roots are steeped in hot water; a formula is recited (W. W.). "...decoction drunk for disease called "black" in which the hands and the eye sockets are said to turn black, also for a disease described as similar to *Unagi·i,* but more dangerous, in which the sockets become black, while the black spots appear on the arms, legs and over the ribs on one side of the body, accompanied by partial paralysis, and resulting in death should the spots appear also on the other side." (2) A tea of wild senna and *C. fasciculata* is taken for fainting spells (A. L.). (3) If you have a sprained arm, try to pull up this plant with it. It can't be done but the arm will be cured (C. S.). (4) Wild senna is one of the ingredients in a medicine for pneumonia (Source forgotten). (5) The leaf is a laxative (M. O.). (6) For high fever in children, give them a root tea of this (A. Sequoyah, Mooney, 1885). (7) A tea for cramps in grownups or children (N. A.). (8) The bruised and moistened root is used to poultice sores (Mooney, 1885).

U na̩ gEiɔnEke i̩, U ta̩ nɔuni gE·i, *(W. W.),* U ni gɔí, *(N. A.),* Gu na gEí, *(M. D.),"black,"* A na gEi, *(A. L.), "big black,"* Di·sta yi, *(C. S.), "they are tough."*

Redbud
Cercis canadensis (L.)

(1) A bark tea for whooping cough (A. L.). (2) Children are fond of eating the blossoms (Witthoft, 1947b).

Kwa ni yu stï, *(A. L.), "like peaches."*

Butterfly Pea
Clitoria mariana (L.)

(1) For sore mouth "thrush" in grownups and babies. Hold the root tea in mouth for 10 - 20 minutes and spit out. Take another mouthful of fresh tea (N. A.).

Tu ya i yuh stï, *(N. A.), "pea-like,"* U na gla del u stï, *(A. L.), "pea, little."*

Crown Vetch
Coronilla varia (L.)

(1) An ingredient in the medicine accompanying Formula 20: "For spoiled saliva caused by dreaming of snakes." (2) Smash the roots, stems, and leaves and rub on for rheumatism or cramps (W. W.). (3) When ballplayers are bathed in a steep of this, it will keep them from getting hurt. An old-time Indian medicine (A. L.).

U nagɔ u sti yu, *(W. W.), "black, little,"*
Uɬ sɔ sta u·tanɔ, *(Olbrecht, 1932),*
Egwɑ ɔsti, *(A. L.). (Introduced)*

Tick Trefoil, Devil's Shoe String
Desmodium nudiflorum (L.) D. C.

(1) Make a tea of the roots and bathe the body for cramps (A. L.). (2) "Get this and as many other 'stick on' plants as you can, including beggar's lice *(Cynoglossum officinale)*, boil, drink and vomit large quantities of it every four days for bad memory. Then you will remember everything" (W. W.).

Tick Trefoil, Devil's Shoe String
Desmodium nudiflorum

U ni ta·lE·i stiɑn dayɑclɑ^{d}gí, *(W. W.), "they come to stick on your clothes,"*

Ski no ka nɑsɑdɔ́, *(A. L.)*

Honey Locust
Gleditsia triacanthos (L.)

(1) An ingredient in the medicine accompanying Formula 46: "For indigestion." (2) Bark tea of honey locust or *Crataegus spp.*, is drunk or bathed in by ball-players to ward off tacklers. "No one wants to run into thorns" (which these plants have) (A. L.). (3) A hot tea of the bark of honey locust and the leaves of *Tovara virginiana* is given to those with whooping cough (N. A.). (4) Beat up the pods fine, make a tea for measles (N. A.).

Ka$^{(+}$shad zi, *(W. W.),* Ka ɫaE^{d}gí, *(T. L., A. L.),* Ka sÈ̀·^{d}gí, *(N. A.), "honey locust."*

Wild Bean
Phaseolus polystachios (L.)

(1) Used in a "green corn" medicine. Will West Long states that a medicine was also drunk by the more conservative families of Big Cove. This medicine passed out of usage about 1895. Leaves and stems of the wild bean were steeped in hot water and the liquor drunk to prevent damage to the stomach by the new beans. No evidence remains of the associated procedure (Olbrecht, 1932). (2) "Let chipmunks collect the roots... raid the chipmunk's den in the fall, replace the stolen beans with corn." The beans are used in bread (T. L.).

A nis$^{(}$ti, *(W. W.), "threads,"* Tu yu ̀yu sti, *(W. W.), "bean-like."*

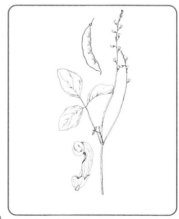

Lupine
Lupinus spp.

(1) Drink and wash with a cold tea made of the entire plant to check hemorrhage and vomiting. Soak head in the tea to stop vomiting (N. A.).

ᴏc·gᴏcli᷄ e gwa᷄, *(N. A.), "...big."*

Pencil Flower, Squaw Vine
Stylosanthes biflora (L.) B. S. P.

(1) A hot tea of the roots is used for female complaint (A. L.). (2) A decoction of the four varieties of *Ga ni gwi li ski: Scutellaria laterflora, S. elliptica, Hypericum spp.*, and *Stylosanthes spp.* is drunk to promote menstruation. The same decoction is also drunk and used as a wash to counteract the ill effects of eating food prepared by a woman in the menstrual condition, or when such a woman by chance comes into a sick room or house under a taboo (Mooney, 1885).

Ga ni gwi li ski, *(A. L.), "clotted blood" or "it is bruised."*

Rabbit Pea, Catgut
Tephrosia virginiana (L.) Pers.

(1) The roots were boiled and the tea was given to children to make them strong and muscular (Olbrecht, 1932). (2) A tea was given to the ball players to transfer the toughness of its root to the muscles (N. A.). The root tea was a ballplayer's remedy. The thighs were scratched and washed with the tea (N. C.). ...Women wash their hair in a decoction of its roots to prevent its breaking or falling out, because these roots are very tough and hard to break. From the same idea ballplayers rub the decoction on their limbs after scratching to toughen them (Mooney, 1885). (3) The decoction is drunk to cure lassitude (Mooney, 1885). (4) The root is used with other ingredients in a medicine for kidney trouble (C. S.). (5) A good medicine for cramps. Scratch the limb and apply a tea made of the root and stem (A. L.).

U ^{dz}a·da li yu sti ga du sa·Ehi, *(N. A.), "pea-like, grows on a mountain,"* Tu yun sti i nEgE·nEhi, *(CS.), "bean, small wild,"* Dis tay, *(Olbrecht, 1932, N. C.),* Al ^{dz}uᴏcnᴏc, *(A. L.).*

Clover
Trifolium pratense (L.)

(1) A tea is made for fevers (H. R.).

Vetch
Vicia caroliniana Walt.

(1) An ingredient in the medicine accompanying
Formula 20: "For spoiled saliva caused by dreaming of
snakes." (2) An ingredient in the medicine accompanying Formula 28: "For local pains, twitching, cramps, etc.
caused by dreams and revengeful animal spirits." (3) The
stem of vetch and the needles of *Pinus virginiana* are
put in a bucket with apple juice and drunk by the ball
players for wind during the game (N. A.). (4) A decoction
is rubbed on the ballplayers after scratching to render
their muscles tough (Mooney, 1885). (5) Rub on a cold
root tea made of the roots and leaves to relieve cramps
(Y. J., Mooney, 1885). (6) An ingredient in a medicine for rheumatism (Mooney, 1885).
"One of the Cherokee's most valuable medicinal herbs."

Aɬ⁺sos ti, (W. W.), Al ᵈᶻɔstɔ, (W. W., T. L., N. A.), *"a wreath for the head,"*
Uɬ tsɔsta us ti ga, (Olbrecht, 1932), *"a wreath for the head, little."*

FLAX FAMILY *Linaceae*

Flax
Linum usitatissimum (L.)

(1) Used in the medicine accompanying Formula 48: "For fever attacks."

DalE·da⁺sut ᵊnɔ, *"washes patient with." (Identified only through common name.) (Introduced)*

WOOD-SORREL FAMILY *Oxalidaceae*

Sorrel
Oxalis spp.

(1) A cold tea will stop vomiting (A. L.). (2) Chew the leaves for "disordered saliva" (when
the saliva tastes bitter and dry—this is not spoiled saliva) (W. W.). (3) Another kind of sorrel
is chewed to cure spoiled saliva (W. W.). (4) Mix a leaf decoction with sheep grease. Put
this salve on sores (L. H.). (5) Make a tea of the entire plant—give to children to drink and
bathe them with it to remove hookworm (A. L.). (6) Good for cancer when it is first started.
Extract the juice from the leaves by wilting and crushing them. Rub the juice on the sores
with the fingers (Y. J.).

Sorrel
Oxalis spp.

^{dj}u ni ^{dj}ɔs ti, *(T. L.),* ^{dj}u ^{dz}ɔis ti, *(W. W.),*
^{dz}u naz oy us ti, *(Y. J.),* ^{dj}u yœs ti, *(C. S.),*
"*sour,*" Gan ^{dz}u?di, *(A. L.).*

GERANIUM FAMILY *Geraniaceae*

Wild Geranium
Geranium maculatum (L.)

(1) It removes things (canker sores) from the gums (M. S.). Steep the leaves and blow the tea into the mouth with a prayer (Mooney, Ms.).

A dan ka la·ski, *(W. W.),* A dan ka la gis ki, *(Mooney, Ms.),* "*it removes things from the gums.*"

MILKWORT FAMILY *Polygalaceae*

Milkwort
Polygala spp. (L.)

(1) A tea of the whole plant or roots is taken for summer complaint (A. L.).

Senega, Seneca Snakeroot
Polygala senega (L.)

(1) For snakebite...Everyone carries in his shot pouch a piece of the best snake root, such as Seneca, or fern snake root, or the wild horse hound, wild plantain, St. Andrew's Cross, and a variety of other herbs and roots, which are plenty... When an Indian perceives he is struck by a snake, he immediately chews some of the root, and having swallowed a sufficient quantity of it he applies some to the wound; which he repeats as the occasion required and in proportion to the poison the snake has injected into the wound (Adair, 1775).

SPURGE FAMILY *Euphorbiaceae*

Ground Milkweed
Euphorbia spp

(1) A cupful of warm tea is given to a mother after the baby is born to stop the bleeding (T. L.).

Ground Milkweed
Euphorbia spp.

Ga ni gwi lis kí, *(T. L.), "clotted blood," or "it is bruised."*

Flowering Spurge, Milkweed
Euphorbia corollata (L.)

(1) An ingredient in the medicine accompanying Formula 6: "For urinary trouble." Make a tea of the bruised stem for glut (white urine). Drink about a pint of the tea early in the morning and again before dinner—take for two or three days (Mooney, Ms.). (2) Put the root in hollowed tooth to stop toothache (Y. J.). Scrape the bark from the root and use for toothache. (3) Put the milky ooze from the stem and leaves on sores and pimples (A. L., N. A., Kimsey Squirrel). Put the milk on warts (M. A.).

U⸢ka tas kis kí, *(Mooney, Ms.),* U gɔctɔcs gis kí, *(A. L.), "pus, it oozes out,"* Gi gɔcgEu'yo du da, *(Y. J.), "blood-like, it is covered,"* U⸢sta gɔcᵈli us ti ga, *(Olbrecht, 1932), "it leaning against, it is little,"* Unɔcdɔci yus ti a tas kis kí, *(N. A.), "milk-like, comes out of."*

Eyebane
Euphorbia maculata (L.)

(1) For when they urinate white. (2) The juice is rubbed on for skin eruption, especially on childrens' heads. Also used for sore nipples (Mooney, 1885). (3) The juice is used as a purgative (Ibid). (4) A decoction is drunk for gonorrhea and similar diseases in both sexes, and is held in high estimation for this purpose (Ibid). (5) The herb is an ingredient in a medicine for cancer.

U gɔctɔcs gis gi, *(Olbrecht, 1932), "pus, it oozes out."*

CASHEW FAMILY *Anacardiaceae*

Dwarf Sumac, Shining Sumac
Rhus copallina (L.)

(1) An ingredient in the medicine accompanying Formula 53: "For water blisters."

Da·lɔni, *(Olbrecht, 1932), "yellow."*

Smooth Sumac
Rhus glabra (L.)

(1) An ingredient in the medicine accompanying Formula 53: "For water blisters." (2) A mother, wishing to raise her child as a witch, fasts her newborn for several days, then drinks a bark decoction that her milk might flow abundantly (Olbrecht, 1932). A cold tea of the roots is used by old women to make their milk flow (T. L.). (3) For convulsions of people and animals when the brain has been affected, a root steep is blown all over the hot areas. A prayer is said (W. W.). (4) Use this and another variety of sumac for "clapps" (gonorrhea). Make a tea of the berries and roots of sumac and the roots of sumac and the root of another herb, drink four times daily (N. A.). (5) The red berries are eaten for kidney trouble or to stop the bedwetting of children (A. L., H. R.). (6) A cold tea of the scraped bark is drunk for bowel trouble (L. H.). (7) Gargle the berry tea for tonsillitis (M. A.). For sores on the arm or mouth during the dog days, make a cold water infusion of the youngest roots of sumac. For young children, lance the blisters with a pin, allowing the water to drain, and rub on the tea (Y. J.).

Kwa l ᵐgᴏ̵, *(A. L.),* Kwa bgᴏ̵, *(W. W., T. L.),* "sumac," Kᴏdo gwᴏs ti yú, *(W. W.),* "sumac small, they are smooth," Kᴏbgwᴣdi dᴏwisᴏgEhi, *(W. W.).*

Poison Ivy
Toxicodendron radicans

(1) An ingredient in the medicine accompanying Formula 54: "For spoiled saliva." Hi gi na li, *(Mooney, Ms.),* "my friend," U ᵈbdá, *(Olbrecht, 1932),* U⁺lᴏdᴏ, *(A. L.).*

Staghorn Sumac
Rhus typhina (L.)

(1) An ingredient in the medicine accompanying Formula 53: "For water blisters."

HOLLY FAMILY *Aquifoliaceae*

American Holly
Ilex opaca Ait.

(1) Scratch muscles with the leaves where sore with cramps (A. L.). (2) The wood is used for carving specialties (Leftwich, 1952). Spoons are made of the wood (Witthoft, 1947b). (3) The berries are used for dye (Witthoft, 1947b).

American Holly
Ilex opaca

Us tas tí, *(A. L., W. W.), "shaking of the top."*

STAFFTREE FAMILY *Celastraceae*

Hearts-a-bustin' with Love, Cat's Paw
Euonymus americanus (L.)

(1) An ingredient in the medicine accompanying Formula 55: "For irregular urination." (2) Boil for a short time the barks of cat's paw, *Liquidambar styraciflua, Vitis aestivalis, Platanus occidentalis, Fagus grandifolia, Smilax glauca,* and *Nyssa sylvatica*—a tea for "bad disease" (T. L.). (3) Drink a root steep at bedtime for "clapps" (gonorrhea). It will be cured in three or four days (T. L.). (4) A warm tea is taken for stomachache (A. L.). (5) Scrape the bark in springtime and make a tea; rub on for cramps in the "veins" (N. A.). (6) Root tea is drunk for falling of the womb (A. L.).

ᵈʲU wᾱdunᾱ, *(A. L.), "they have sinews, they are big."*

MAPLE FAMILY *Aceraceae*

Red Maple
Acer rubrum (L.)

(1) Steep and boil the bark; drink the tea for dysentery (W. W.). (2) The inner bark is boiled into a heavy syrup and made into pills. These are dissolved in water which is used as an eyewash for sore eyes (Witthoft, 1947b). (3) Drink the tea when people have red spots (hives) (A. L.). (4) Boil the bark and steam the eyes to help blindness (T. L.). (5) A steep of the barks of four trees is a good medicine for monthly female trouble: red maple, *Quercus alba, Q. nigra,* and *Castenea dentata* (Y. J.).

Red Maple
Acer rubrum

Tehu na wa kí, *(W. W.),* ^{h}Lu ha wa kí, *(W. W.),* Tchɑwa gɑ́, *(N. A.),* ^{d}Su wa gí, *(T. L.),* ^{k}Lɑwɑgí, *(Olbrecht, 1932),* *"blood-like, it is a flower,"* Gi gɑgÉa^{dz}i lɑ·skí, *(A. L.),* *"red maple."*

Silver Maple
Acer saccharinum (L.)

(1) Hot bark tea taken for measles (Amonite Sequoyah).

(Some of the Cherokee names for A. rubrum, above, doubtless apply also to other maples.)

BUCKEYE FAMILY *Hippocastanaceae*

Buckeye
Aesculus pavia (L.)

(1) An ingredient in the medicine accompanying Formula 46: "For indigestion." (2) The nuts are pounded and used in a poultice (Witthoft, 1947b). Scrape the meat out of a nut and make a salve for sores (N. C., A. L.). (3) Carry a nut in your pocket to cure piles (N. C.). (4) When a person feels queer, as if he is going to faint or as if a fit is coming on, scrape out some of the meat of a nut, grind it into a flour, and steep it in warm water. Drink (W. W.). (5) A bark tea is drunk by pregnant women to facilitate delivery (A. L.). (6) Sometimes women, after giving birth to a baby, won't stop

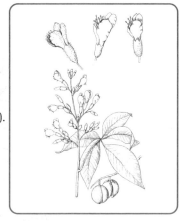

bleeding and they take cramps. Prepare a cold infusion of the barks of buckeye and *Castanea dentata* and give them to drink. "...not too much or it will stop everything" (Y. J.). (7) Buckeye wood is used in carving. It was a favorite wood in carving large dishes (A. L.). (8) The bark is used as a fish poison (Willhoft, 1947b). (9) Small pieces of the nut are chewed, and the juice is swallowed for colic (M. O.).

Us kwɑt'i, Unis kwɑdá, *(W. W.),* Os kwa dá, *(A. L.),* U nis kwu tú, *(W. W.),* Ga la gEná akɑtɑ, *(M. O.),* *"buckeye,"* *(the last Cherokee name cited is a literal translation, "buck eye," the preceding are Cherokee proper names.) (Identification by Olbrecht).*

TOUCH-ME-NOT FAMILY *Balsaminaceae*

Orange or Spotted Touch-me-not
Impatiens capensis Meerb.

(1) An ingredient in the green corn medicine with *Andropogon virginicus, Zea mays,* and *Cucurbita pepo* (M. S.). In a second green corn medicine (see appendix) it is an alternate ingredient (W. W.). (2) A decoction including the stem of touch-me-not, the cone of *Pinus pungens,* the root of *Veronica officinalis,* and the bark of *Ulmus rubra* is given to pregnant women before going into the water each new moon. Touch-me-not is used because the exploding character of the ripe fruits is believed to expedite delivery (Olbrecht, 1932). The woman's vulva is bathed with a warm decoction of touch-me-not if delivery is difficult (Olbrecht, 1932, N. C., M. S.). Make a tea of the stalks. Beginning in her sixth month of pregnancy, a mother will drink this tea every day until her child is born (Y. J.). (3) Crush the leaves in hand and rub on a child's stomach for sourness (A. L.). (4) A leaf tea is drunk for measles (H. R.). (5) A root tea is drunk for "bold hives" in babies (M. A.). (6) Rub the leaves on body to cure "poison oak" (L. H.). (7) The blossoms are used in making an apricot dye for fabric (Leftwich, 1952).

Wa lElú unig lEgis tí, *(N. C.),* Wa lElú una dzi la gis tí, *(N. C.), "shaking of the top."*

Yellow Touch-me-not
Impatiens pallida Nutt.

While a few medicines call for a specific color of touch-me-not to be used as an ingredient, there is little uniformity. Apparently W. W. recognized a difference in the two touch-me-nots, but A. L., for one, draws no line of distinction, and considers them the same plant. The writer accepts the later view as the most common, and believes that the Cherokee names and usages for *I. capensis* are, on the whole, applicable to yellow touch-me-not. In (1) above, Olbrecht quotes W. W. as specifying *I. capensis.*

BUCKTHORN FAMILY *Rhamnaceae*

New Jersey Tea
Ceanothus americanus (L.)

(1) When "tired in the chest," drink as much of the warm tea as you can and vomit (T. L.). T. L. adds that when the flowers of this plant are out, snakes are most apt to strike. (2) Take the root and make a hot tea for bowel complaint. Drink before bedtime (N. A., A. L.).

New Jersey Tea
Ceanothus americanus

E·lis ʻgɑ╳lɑ́, *(N. A., T. L., N. C.),* E lis ʻkaɨ, *(A. L.).*

VINE FAMILY *Vitaceae*

Possum Grape
Ampelopsis cordata Michx.

(1) An ingredient in the medicine accompanying Formula: 55 "For irregular urination."
(2) An ingredient in the medicine accompanying Formula: 78 "For bad diarrhea."

U nɑ́suga, *(Olbrecht, 1932), "toes in the liquid."*

Summer Grape
Vitis aestivalis Michx.

(1) An ingredient in the medicine accompanying Formula 55: "For irregular urination." (2) An ingredient in the medicine accompanying Formula: 78 "For bad diarrhea." (3) Boil for a short time the barks of summer grape, *Euonymus americanus, Liquidambar styraciflua, Platanus occidentalis, Fagus grandifolia, Smilax glauca,* and *Nyssa sylvatica*—a tea for "bad disease" (T. L.). (4) The grapes are eaten as food (T. L.).

TE·lo dí, *(Olbrecht, 1932),* TElɑa dí, *(T. L.),* TElɑ́·lɑdi, *(A. L.), "it hangs down."*

Fox Grape
Vitis labrusca (L.)

(1) An ingredient in the medicine accompanying Formula 55: "For irregular urination." (2) The grapes are eaten for food (W. W.).

Fox Grape
Vitis labrusca

Te lɔchɔdí, *(W. W.)*, *"berries hanging on,"*
Kwɔ ᵈtu·si, *(Olbrecht, 1932)*, Kwa lu sɔ́,
(W.W.), *"blisters."*

BASSWOOD FAMILY *Tiliaceae*

American Basswood
Tilia americana (L.)

(1) An ingredient in the medicine accompanying Formula 49: "For diarrhea." (2) Chew on the bark and spit the juice on a snakebite. The tree must be one struck by lightning (Mooney, Ms.). Beat the bark and make a cold tea for snakebite. "They've used it for dogs." Drink and bathe in it (A. L.). (3) An infusion drunk for the cure of a type of tuberculosis caused by incantation includes the barks of basswood, *Quercus spp.*, *Castanea dentata*, *Carya spp.*, *Fagus grandifolia*, and *Liriodendron tulipifera* (W. W.). (4) The wood is used for carving. (5) Beat the bark and make a poultice for boils (M. A.).

I dɔha *(A. L.)*, I dEhɔ, *(Olbrecht, 1932)*, I·tEha *(W. W.)*, *"basswood."*

White Basswood
Tilia heterophylla Vent.

The dried specimen which the writer used for his work with various informants was the leaf of a cultivated basswood, which, of course, was not native to the area. Each informant recognized it immediately as a basswood and gave a name for it, but a few persons remarked that it looked "different." The writer concludes that no distinctions are drawn between the several species of basswood (other than habitat location) and that the Cherokee name and usage for *T. heterophylla*, above, applies also to white basswood.

ST. JOHN'S WORT FAMILY *Clusiaceae*

St. Peter's Wort, St. Andrew's Cross, Feeble Weed *Hypericum hypericoides* (L.)

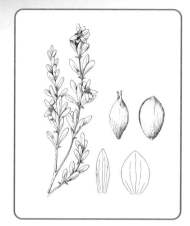

(1) To give babies strength, bathe them in a warm or cold root tea. "Some babies will walk at eight or nine months with this" (N. A.). (2) Make a tea with as much as you can hold in your hand. To break a fever, drink this and go to bed (A. L.). (3) For snakebite (see *Polygala senega*) (Adair, 1775).

Ga ni gwa lis kí a ya tœli, *(W. W.)*, *"clotted blood, flat on ground,"* Dis ta yi, *(N. A., A. L.).*

St. John's Wort, Flux Weed *Hypericum perforatum* (L.)

(1) The top leaves are made into a tea for bloody flux (H. R.). Beat the roots fine and make a cold root tea. Drink as much as you can for bowel complaint (N. A.). (2) A decoction of the four varieties of *Ga ni gwi lis ki Scutellaria lateriflora, S. elliptica, Hypericum spp.,* and *Stylosanthes spp.* is drunk to promote menstruation, and the same decoction is also drunk and used as a wash to counteract the ill effects of eating food prepared by a woman in the menstrual condition, or when such a woman by chance comes into a sick room or house under a taboo (Mooney, 1885).

Gi ga ^{dj}u ya i, *(N. A.), "blood, it has them in it,"* Gœni gwa^{d}lis ki, *(Olbrecht, 1932), "clotted blood," "it is bruised." (Introduced)*

ROCKROSE FAMILY *Cistaceae*

Frostweed *Helianthemum spp.*

(1) Steep the leaves of either of these in cold water, drink for kidney trouble (M. S.).

GEg^{no} wEdo widɔ, *(M. S.).*

VIOLET FAMILY *Violaceae*

Pansy Violet, Johnny Jump Up
Viola pedata (L.)

(1) Crush the root and make a poultice for boils (M. A.).

Den das d∝skí, *(N. C.)*.

Round Leaved Violet
Viola rotundifolia Michx.

(1) Beat the root fine and make a tea to doctor corn with before planting. Keeps insects from destroying the corn.

Di n∝das k∝dE·skí, *(A. L.)*, Ka nEs'í, *(N. A.)*, An da, *(T. T.)*.

PASSION FLOWER FAMILY *Passifloraceae*

Passion Flower, Apricot Vine
Passiflora incarnata (L.)

(1) The fruit is edible (T. L.). Boil the fruit until syrupy, or eat raw. For a drink, crush the fruit, remove the seeds and mix the pulp with water (C. S.). (2) It is just like the apricot, but it has a small non-edible berry. For brier locust wounds, pound the root and apply to the sores. It will draw out the inflammation (W. W.). One of the ingredients in a root tea for boils (N. A.). (3) Beat up the root in warm water, drop into ear for earache (A. L.). (4) For babies who are hard to wean, make a tea of the roots and give to the six-month-old baby. At one year the baby will "drop off the breast" as an apricot drops off the vine (N. A.).

Ne skwe tu kí, *(C. S.)*, *"apricot,"* U w∝ga, *(N. A.)*, U·wa ga, *(N. C., A. L., T. L.)*.

SORGHUM FAMILY *Nyssaceae*

Black Gum
Nyssa sylvatica Marsh.

(1) An ingredient in the medicine accompanying Formula 34: "For when the stomach is yellow." (2) An ingredient in the medicines accompanying Formula 38: "For urinary diffi-culty." (3) An ingredient in the medicine accompanying Formula 78: "For diarrhea." A bark steep is drunk for dysentery (W. W.). (4) Boil for a short time the barks of black gum, *Euonymus americanus, Vitis aestivalis, Liquidambar styraciflua, Platanus occidentalis, Fagus grandifolia* and *Smilax glauca*—a tea for bad disease (T. L.). (5) Make a strong root ooze for the eyes. Wrap the ooze in a cloth and allow it to drip into the eyes (A. L.).

Black Gum
Nyssa sylvatica

(6) A root tea is given by midwives to pregnant women to facilitate delivery, "it gets the pains to working right" (H. R.). (7) Cut up the bark and make a tea for "flooding" (excessive bleeding) in women (M. A.).

U ni gwa, *(W. W.),* U ni kwa, *(A. L.),* *"black gum."*

EVENING PRIMROSE FAMILY *Onagraceae*

Evening Primrose, Hog Weed
Oenothera spp.

(1) Eat the greens when young (T. L.). (2) Beat the roots fine, heat them, and make a poultice for piles (T. L.).

An dɔsɔ Egwa, *(T. L.), "dig trout,"* Si kwa U ni gis ti, *"the hog eats it."*

GINSENG FAMILY *Araliaceae*

Sarsaparilla
Aralia nudicaulis (L.)

(1) Drink the root tea for the blood (A. L.).

Spikenard
Aralia racemosa (L.)

(1) Drink a root tea for backache, kidneys and lumbago (M. A., H. R., A. L.).

Devil's Walking Stick, Angelica Tree
Aralia spinosa (L.)

(1) Make a salve of the roots for old sores (A. L.). (2) Bathe in a root ooze to cure paralysis (A. L.). (3) A decoction of the roasted and pounded roots is given as an emetic. It is very

Devil's Walking Stick, Angelica Tree
Aralia spinosa

strong; green it is poisonous (Witthoft, 1947b).

U^dza ki dá, *(A. L.),* Yɔnɔͼuni^{hi}ya gis ti, *(T. L.).*

Dwarf Ginseng
Panax trifolius (L.)

(1) An ingredient in the medicines accompanying Formula 2 and 82: "For headache." (2) For breast pains. (3) An ingredient in the medicine accompanying Formula 42: "For fits, apoplexy." (4) Along with other ingredients, a tea is made for "bad hives," a childrens' disease that will bring death in two or three hours. (5) "A root which never fails curing the most inveterate venereal disease" (Timberlake). (6) Take a tea of the roots as stomach medicine (A. L.). (7) Chew the root for short breath, coughing (T. L.). Take a bite of the root every noon, and swallow (N. A.). (8) Chew the

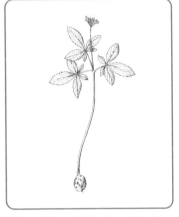

roots for colic, or make a hot water infusion (H. R., M. A.). Chew the root for sore side (L. H.). (9) Beat the roots of ginseng and *Erythronium americanum* and make a cold infusion which is good for fainting persons (Y. J.). The herb is one which is stored by medicine men, rather than collected only when needed (Olbrecht, 1932).

O da li ga li, *(T. L.),* Gun sti ga, *(M. S.), "mountain, he climbs,"* ɔda li gɔͼ^dti A ta li ga li, *(N. C.),* ɔdɔͼli gɔͼli, *(A. L., N. A.).*

Ginseng, Sang
Panax quinquefolius (L.)

(1) A poultice of the beaten roots is used for boils (M. A.). (2) A decoction of the root is drunk for headaches, cramps, etc., and for female trouble (Mooney, 1885). (3) The chewed root is blown on the sore spot for the pains in the side (Mooney, 1885). The Cherokee sell large quantities of "sang" to the traders for fifty cents per pound, nearly equivalent to two day's wages, a fact which has doubtless increased their idea of its importance (Ibid).

Ginseng, Sang
Panax quinquefolius
The Cherokee name and usages for this and P. trifolius
are believed to be approximately the same. In a few
cases the informant specified "small" or "large" 'sang.'

PARSLEY FAMILY *Apiaceae*

Water Parsnip
Angelica venenosa Greenway Fern.

(1) Wash hands with a leaf infusion seven days after
handling a corpse (T. L.). (2) A tea is drunk by
pregnant women (A. L.).

G∝nEɬ da, *(T. L.)*, G nÈ lEda, *(A. L.).*

Poison Hemlock
Cicuta maculata (L.)

(1) A plant the old timers used to find out how long
they would live. They would chew the roots, if they
got dizzy they would die soon—if not, they would live a
long time (A. L.). (2) The root is chewed and swallowed
for four days consecutively by women who wish to
become sterile (Olbrecht, 1932). (This information may
have been given to Olbrecht who was over-zealous in
obtaining information of an intimate nature.) This was
possibly a little joke played on Olbrecht, who was
unaware of the poisonous quality of the plant. (3) It
kills what eats it. Corn is soaked in a root tea before

planting to repel insect pests (H. R.).

Ti li yus ti, *(Olbrecht, 1932), "chestnut-like,"* Kɔ̄na so la, *(T. L.).*

Button Snakeroot, Rattlesnake Master
Eryngium yuccifolium Michx.

(1) Used in the medicine accompanying Formula 50:
"For stomach trouble caused by bad odors." (2) "White
folks used it for string to tie up hog meat" (A. L.).
(3) A root tea is held in the mouth for toothache
(M. A.). (4) A decoction is given to children to prevent
them from catching whooping cough (Olbrecht, 1932).

U wEti, *(Olbrecht, 1932),* SEla kwɔ·yɔ̄, *(T. L.),*
SE·li kwɔ·ya, *(Olbrecht, 1932).*

Cow Bane, Wild Potato
Oxypolis rigidior (L.) C & R

(1) The root is baked and eaten (T. L.).

Nu na a go da nEi, *(T. L.).*

Wild Parsnip
Pastinaca sativa (L.)

(1) An ingredient in the medicine accompanying
Formula 3: "For sharp pains." (2) The root of wild
parsnip and the bark of *Oxydendrum arboreum* are
boiled in a pot over a fire in which is burning some
rubbish from around the house of a deceased person.
The conjuror who was unsuccessful in saving the life
of the dead person washes his hands in the pot for
purification (Olbrecht, 1932).

Kɔ̄nɔsɔ^{cu}lɔ, *(Olbrecht, 1932). (Introduced)*

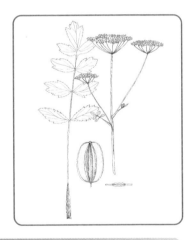

Black Snakeroot
Sanicula spp.

(1) Steep the root, drink for stomach trouble (A. L.). A tea is drunk for colic (H. R.).

U lEukɔ̄łdi, *(W. W.), "treed by the locust."*

Golden Alexander
Zizia aurea (L.) W. D. J. Koch

(1) The root is chewed by medicine man initiates when in danger of coming in contact with a pregnant woman.

GɔcnE·ɫdɔ́, *(W. W.), "it is pregnant."*

DOGWOOD FAMILY *Cornaceae*

Dogwood
Cornus florida (L.)

(1) An ingredient in the medicine accompanying Formula 21: "For aggravated hoarseness." (2) Used in the medicine accompanying Formula 78: "For bad diarrhea." (3) Boil together the barks of dogwood, *Prunus serotina,* and *Lindera benzoin.* This tea, added to pure corn whiskey, is drunk to break out the measles (A. L.). A bark tea is taken for the measles (N. A.). (4) The petals boiled in water is taken for colds (M. A.). (5) The bark is chewed for headache (C. S.). Bathe in a tea made of the beaten bark for poison of any kind (N. A.). Make a poultice of the bark for "oak poison." The bark is used in poultices (Witthoft, 1947b). (7) The bark of the root is used to heal wounds (Witthoft, 1947b). (8) For chicken pox, make a decoction of the bark of an old tree—pour the warm water over the body and bathe in it. The pox will clear up the same day, but scars may remain (W. W.).

KɔcnE?sitɔ́c, *(L. S.),* Ka nu?si tá, *(W. W.),* Gɔcna^{dz} iɔt́, *(A. L.),* Ka na si tá, *(T. L.),* Kɔcnu si tɔ́c, *(N. A.).*

WHITE ALDER FAMILY *Clethraceae*

White Alder
Clethra acuminata Michx.

(1) An ingredient in the medicine accompanying Formula 15 and 34: "For disordered bile." (2) A hot bark infusion is good for bowel complaint (Y. J.). (3) A decoction of the barks of white alder and *Prunus serotina* is drunk to break a high fever (A. L.).

Su lù·yiɫ^{u}gá, *(Olbrecht, 1932), "swamp tree,"* D dɔcnElɔcwɔski, *(A. L.), "peels off," (note that these names are identical to those of Hydrangea arborescens).*

WINTERGREEN FAMILY *Pyrolaceae*

Spotted Wintergreen
Chimaphila maculata (L.) Pursh.

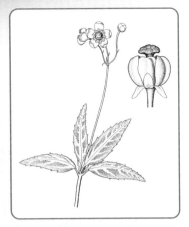

(1) Wash the roots until white, beat them up and make a poultice for headaches or any kind of pain (N. A.). (2) Make a tea of the tops and roots for colds and LaGrippe (M. A.). Drink a root tea if feverish inside (A. L.). A tea for colds and fever (H. R.). (3) Drink a tea for women's pains (A. L.).

U stas ti, *(A. L.)*, U stas ti u di yɔ̄, *(W. W.),* *"twisting little,"* Anɔ̄skwa lɔ̄ski, *(N. A.).*

Indian Pipe
Monotropa uniflora (L.)

(1) Make an infusion of the whole plant in cold water and use for sore eyes (A. L.). (A. L. says that the appearance of the first "wart" is sign that frost is three months away.) (2) Indian Pipe "grows like a mushroom," it is a sacrophytic flowering plant, devoid of chlorophyll. Mash up the whole plant and rub on to cure bunions or warts (N. A.).

Wɔlɔ·si nu wɔti, *(N. A.), "wart medicine,"* Dɔ̄wɔ·li, *(W. W.), "wart." (?)*

HEATH FAMILY *Ericaceae*

Trailing Arbutus
Epigaea repens (L.)

(1) Used in the medicine accompanying Formula 17: "For diarrhea." (2) An ingredient in the medicine accompanying Formula 54: "For abdominal pains caused by the terrapin." (3) A tea is made for chest ailment. In summertime the roots and leaves are used; in winter only the roots are used (N. A.). (4) A root tea is drunk for kidney trouble. (M. A.) (5) The roots of "ground hog's forehead" and *Gaultheria procumbens* are made into a tea for chronic indigestion (M. S.).

Trailing Arbutus
Epigaea repens

Dɔ?siᵘwɔyi, *(N. A.),* Do ka shí go⁺si⁺si,
(M. S.), "terrapin's foot," Oɔg nú a gɔda gÉ,
(M. S.), "ground hog's head."

Teaberry, Wintergreen
Gaultheria procumbens (L.)

(1) The roots of "it smells, it little" and *Epigaea repens*
are make into a tea for chronic indigestion (M. S.).
(2) The dried leaves of the "black bush herb" are a
substitute for chewing tobacco (W. W.).

Asᵘ giˊli yuˊsti, *(W. W., M. S.), "it smells, it
little,"* A⁺ɔgi gɔnun la hí, *(W. W.), "black
bush herb."*

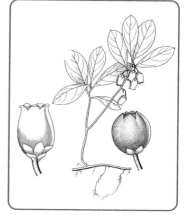

Mountain Laurel
Kalmia latifolia (L.)

(1) An ingredient in the medicine accompanying
Formula 31: "For muscle soreness." (2) An ingredient
in the medicine accompanying Formula 36: "For
shifting pains." (3) A leaf decoction including the
leaves of mountain laurel, *Rhododendron maximum*,
and *Leucothoe editorum* is applied to rheumatic areas
for relief (A. L., Sevier Crowe). (4) Take all possible
laurels and some other plants and steep. Rub this tea
on for rheumatism, after scratching first with scratcher
(W. W.). Peel and boil the stick; rub on this tea for
rheumatism (N. C., M. S.). (4) In old times a leaf ooze

was rubbed into the scratched skin of the ballplayers to prevent cramps (A. L.). (5) Of the leaves a salve was made for healing (Amonite Sequoyah). (6) The leaves were used for surgical scratching (Olbrecht, 1932).

Du shu ga´ ᵈʲun sti ya´, *(W. W.),* Du su? ᵈʲun sti´, *(A. L., N. C., T. L., N. A.),* "*laurel, it small,*" Dus u?go, *(M. S.),* "*laurel.*"

Dog Hobble
Leucothoe fontainesiana Fern & Schub.

(1) An ingredient in the medicine accompanying Formula 31: "For muscle soreness." (2) An ingredient in the medicine accompanying Formula 36: "For shifting pains." (3) A leaf decoction including the leaves of dog hobble, *Kalmia latifolia,* and *Rhododendron maximum* is applied to rheumatic areas for relief (A. L., Sevier Crowe). (4) Apply an ooze made of the beaten-up roots to dogs to cure them of mange (A. L.). (5) For itch, take a bath in some water in which has been poured a decoction of the leaf and stem. "Indians get it...it is caused by uncleanliness" (M. A.).

E· ᵘsɔ´, *(Olbrecht, 1932),* E wa su hi´, *(Olbrecht, 1932),* E?was uhi´, *(A. L.),* "*dog hobble.*"

Sourwood
Oxydendrum arboreum (L.) D. C.

(1) An ingredient in the medicine accompanying Formula 38: "For urinary trouble." (2) An ingredient in the medicine accompanying Formula 78: "For bad diarrhea." The young shoots are scraped and the bark is stewed for diarrhea—especially in the winter (W. W.). A cold bark steep will check the bowels of children (Y. J.). Beat up the leaves in cold water for diarrhea (Y. J.). (3) The twigs of sourwood and the root of *Pastinaca sativa* are boiled in a pot over a fire which is burning some rubbish from around the house of a deceased person. The conjuror who was unsuccessful in saving the life of the dead person washes his hands in the pot for purification (Olbrecht, 1932). (4) A taboo is placed on the burning of sourwood for fuel because the burning of it will cause sickness (Olbrecht, 1932). (5) For itch, take a bath in some water in which has been poured a decoction of the bark (M. A.). (6) Sourwood branches were used in the making of arrows (John Witthoft).

N d gwE ya´, *(Olbrecht, 1932),* Na dogwa ya´, *(A. L.),* NɔcdɔgwEyɔc, *(T. L.),* NadwgwE yɔc, *(A. L.),* "*sourwood.*"

Flame Azalea
Rhododendron calendulaceum Michx. Torr.

(1) Peel and boil a twig and rub the twig on the place
of rheumatism (M. S.). (2) A fungus "apple" formed on
the stems is eaten to appease thirst when in the
mountains (C. S.). (3) The flowers are used to decorate
the house (A. L.).

Kɔna giɔs ki, *(C. S., A. L.), "turkey beard,"*
Dus'u?go, *(W. W.), "laurel."*

Great Rhododendron
Rhododendron maximum (L.)

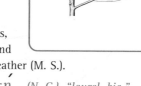

(1) An ingredient in the medicine accompanying
Formula 31: "For muscle soreness." (2) An ingredient
in the medicine accompanying Formula 36: "For
shifting pains." (3) A leaf decoction including the
leaves of "laurel, big," *Kalmia latifolia,* and *Leucothoe
editorum* is applied to rheumatic areas for relief (A. L.,
Sevier Crowe). The above decoction also rubbed on
the scratches of ballplayers (A. L.). Peel and boil a
twig and rub the twig on the place of rheumatism
(M. S.). (4) The wood is used in carving (spoons, toys,
etc.) (N. C.). (5) Throw clumps of leaves into a fire and
dance around it (a social dance) to bring on cold weather (M. S.).

Dus'ugɔ^{dj}un tɔnɔ, *(C. S.),* Dusu?^{dz}un tɔn , *(N. C.), "laurel, big."*

DIAPENSIA FAMILY *Diapensiaceae*

Galax, Horse Hoof
Galax aphylla (L.)

(1) A root for kidney trouble (Y. J.).

Dɔ?sɔwa i, *(A. L.), "terrapin foot,"* Di gasɔcgwɔclɔcu^{dj}wa lo gi, *(T. L.),*
Sɔgwili ^{u}la si di, *(Y. J.).*

PRIMROSE FAMILY *Primulaceae*

Whorled Loosestrife
Lysimachia quadrifolia (L.)

(1) An ingredient in the medicine accompanying Formula 55: "For when they urinate white." A cold infusion is sometimes good for yellow urine (M. S.). The root is used as a diuretic. A. L.'s grandfather was taken sick in the mountains. For relief he ate this plant from the palm of his hand and drank water (A. L.). A kidney medicine (N. C.). (2) A tea for female trouble (T. L.). (3) For children and grownups who pass blood and pus with their bowels, make a cold root tea (Source unknown).

Gi ga⁺su yá, *(Olbrecht, 1932),* Gi gꝏ^dz^u ya í, *(N. C., A. L., T. L.), "blood in your veins," "blood, it has taken in it,"* Dꝏbní, *(M. S., N. A.), "yellow."*

EBONY FAMILY *Ebenaceae*

Persimmon
Diospyros virginiana (L.)

(1) An ingredient in the medicine accompanying Formula 72: "For flux." (2) Used in the medicine accompanying Formula 84: "For rheumatism." (3) An ingredient in the medicine accompanying Formula 86: "For indigestion." (4) Chew the bark for heartburn (A. L.). (5) The wood was used to carve disease stampers in ancient times (Olbrecht, 1932). (6) Used with another plant for toothache (N. A.). For toothache make a warm or cold infusion of several barks: persimmon, *Alnus serrulata, Juglans cinerea,* and *Prunus serotina.* "Hold the tea in your mouth against the decayed tooth and the pus will come to a head" (N. A.).

Su lí, *(Olbrecht, 1932),* Sꝏlí, *(A. L.),* Sa lí, *(N. A.).*

LOGANIA FAMILY *Loganiaceae*

Indian Pink
Spigelia marilandica (L.)

(1) An ingredient in the medicine accompanying Formulas 32 and 52: "For intestinal worms."
Gi gꝏgÉ a^dz^ilɔskí, *(Olbrecht, 1932), "bloodlike, it has flowers."*

DOGBANE FAMILY *Apocynaceae*

Indian Hemp
Apocynum cannabinum (L.)

(1) Beat up, make a poultice for rheumatism (Lloyd Lambert). (2) The fibers are used for bow strings, mask cords, etc. (W. W.). (3) The fibers are used to weave grave cloth material (Olbrecht, 1932). (4) The roots are boiled and strained and taken to clean out the kidneys (for Bright's disease) (M. O.).

An do la kœ, *(W. W.), "they have broken legs,"* Ga da lu di, Ga dœladœ, *(W. W.), "broke my leg."*

MILKWEED FAMILY *Asclepiadaceae*

Milkweed
Asclepias perennis Walt.

(1) Peel off the bark, smooth it, twist it for bowstring (A. L.). (2) A warm infusion of this milkweed and *Clematis virginiana* is drunk for backache, or the roots may be chewed instead. Salt is forbidden (T. L.).

Us ti ga li, *(T. C.),* Ga do bda, *(A. L.).*

Butterfly Weed, Pleurisy Root
Asclepias tuberosa (L.)

(1) Make a tea of the beaten up root for diarrhea. Drink all you can (A. L., N. C.). A tea for diarrhea. If there are a lot of the butterflies around the flowers, the plant is good for medicine, otherwise it is not. The butterflies must be the same color as the blossoms (W. W., M. S.). For bloody flux in grownups or children, make a decoction and drink while warm (N. A.). (2) A tea is drunk for pleurisy (N. C., A. L., M. A.). (3) A root tea is taken for heart trouble (H. R.). (4) A root tea for fever (H. R.). (5) The stem is used in making belts (John Witthoft).

Butterfly Weed, Pleurisy Root
Asclepias tuberosa

Gu·gu, *(W. W., M. S., A. L.)*, *"bottle" or "chigger"*
Gig∝su ya i, *(N. A.)*, OnEskwɔhi, *(N. A.)*.

CONVOLVULUS FAMILY *Convolvulaceae*

Sweet Potato Vine, Trumpet Vine
Ipomoea pandurata (L.) G. F. W. Meg.

(1) Drink a tea for "cholera morbis" (bowel complaint)
(H. R.). (2) The old Indians made a tea out of the vine
to treat sweet potatoes before setting them out. The tea
was put in a tub in which the young plants were soaked
before transplanting. This keeps away the bugs and
moles (N. A.). (3) The bark of the root is scraped off and
wrapped in muslin for a poultice used to relieve
rheumatic pains. The moist poultice is kept on for a
period of 15 to 20 minutes (Narcissa Owen, 1907).

Nu na u ga nas ta i yuh sti, *(N. A.)*,
"potatoes, sweet-like."

POLEMONIUM FAMILY *Polemoniaceae*

Sweet William
Phlox maculata (L.)

(1) To make children grow and fatten, bathe in a root infusion (N. C.).
Ga d∝^{dz}us li, *(N. C.)*.

Creeping Phlox
Phlox stolonifera Sims.

(1) An ingredient in the medicine accompanying Formula 75: "For chills."

⁺su w∝du·na us ti ga, *(Olbrecht, 1932)*, *"it has sinews, it small,"* Du su go Ei,
(?), *"laurel, is living."*

BORAGE FAMILY *Boraginaceae*

Beggar's Lice
Cynoglossum virginianum (L.)

(1) An ingredient in the medicine accompanying Formula 4: "For itching." (2) An alternate ingredient in the green corn medicine (see Appendix). (3) For kidney trouble when the urine is white—the root is boiled four times into a thick syrup. This decoction is taken for four days during which the patient abstains from all food containing salt. The root is generally collected in the summer while the top is green because the root must be pulled up by the tops, not dug (Mooney, Ms.). (4) The root is used for cancer (Ibid). (5) Take this and other "stick on" plants and make a decoction to be drunk every four days for bad memory. "Then you will remember everything" (W. W.).

U nis ti bi´ stiΕgwɔ, *(Olbrecht, 1932), "they make them stick to it, the little one,"*

U nis ti lu is ti, *(Mooney, Ms.), "something that sticks to the clothes."*

Blueweed, Blue Devil
Echium vulgare (L.)

(1) For when they urinate white.

U nis kɔi´, *(Olbrecht, 1932), "their heads."*

Stickseed
Lappula spp.

(1) An ingredient in the medicine accompanying Formula 4: "For itching."

U nis ti bis tiΕgu`, *(Olbrecht, 1932), "they make them stick to it."*

Puccoon
Lithospermum spp.

(1) The seeds were used as conjurer's beads (W. W.).

U ni·s ko´, *(W. W.), "beads."*

MINT FAMILY *Lamiaceae*

Wood Mint
Blephilia spp.

(1) A poultice of the leaves is used for headache (N. A.). (N. A. uses all "*gows gi*" plants for headaches.)

Gowsɔgi´, *(N. A.), "it smells."*

Horse Balm
Collinsonia canadensis (L.)

(1) Used in the medicine accompanying Formula 29: "For swollen breasts." (2) Rub the leaves and flowers between hands and apply as poultice to the armpits to prevent excessive odor there (W. W.).

Di ga ya su gi, *(W. W.), "arm pit smell."*

Ground Ivy
Glechoma hederacea (L.)

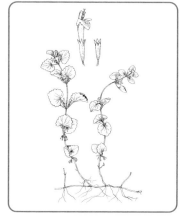

(1) A tea is given to babies for hives (A. L., H. R.). Steep the leaves in hot water, drink for measles (W. W.).

Gɔws'u gi, *(N. A.), "it smells,"* Ga wasɔcgi u dɔcni si ni do?, *(W. W.), "vine on the ground, shaking itself."*

Pennyroyal
Hedeoma pulegioides (L.) Pers.

(1) Beat the leaves and put in mouth for toothache (T. L.). (2) Rub the leaves on the body to repel insect pests (Sevier Crowe, Y. J., H. R.). (3) A cold tea of the leaves or the entire plant is drunk for the flux (Y. J., Betty Owle). (4) A tea of the entire plant is taken for colds (A. L., H. R., M. A., L. H., Betty Owle). (5) A tea of the leaves and stem is drunk for fever (M. A., Betty Owle). (6) Beat up the leaves and apply as poultice to relieve headaches (N. A.).

Gowsɔcgi, *(N. A., N. C., A. L., T. L.), "it smells."*

Water Horehound
Lycopus virginicus (L.)

(1) A tea of this plant is drunk at a green corn ceremony (Witthoft, 1947b). (2) The root is chewed and given to infants to gnaw on to give them eloquence of speech (W. W.). (3) Wring the plant in sweet milk, boil for five minutes, and feed to a dog which has been snakebitten (L. H.).

A ni wa nis ki, *(W. W.).*

Peppermint
Mentha spicata (L.)

(1) Drink a cold infusion for sick stomach (M. A.). Wring up the leaves in water and drink for upset stomach (H. R.). (2) Drink a tea to depress fevers (Witthoft, 1947b). (3) Smell the leaves to relieve colds (Witthoft, 1947b). (4) The plant is used to flavor foods and medicine (H. R.).

Gow sɔgi, *(A. L., N. A.), "it smells,"*
Wes da?u ni gEs ti, *(Witthoft, 1947b), "cat eats."*

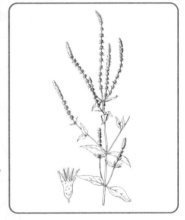

Horsemint
Monarda spp.

(1) A poultice of the leaves is applied for headache (T. L., N. A.). (2) "When I was a boy it was gathered in large bundles to hang up...it was used for colds" (Jess Lambert).

Gw'sɔch gi, *(T. L.),* Gon sɔdi, *(W. W.), "it smells."*

Crimson Beebalm, Oswego Tea, Red Horsemint
Monarda didyma (L.)

(1) To stop nose bleed, sniff an infusion made of the crushed leaves (Y. J.). To stop nose bleed, dampen the head with and drink a cold root infusion (N. A.). (2) A hot leaf tea brought out the measles when everything else failed (Cam Sneed).

Crimson Beebalm, Oswego Tea, Red Horsemint *Monarda didyma*

Gows∝gi, *(N. A.), "it smells,"* Gi g∝gE
a^{dj}i lus ki, *(Y. J., N. A.), "blood-like, it has flowers."*

Wild Bergamot
Monarda fistulosa (L.)

(1) A warm poultice will relieve headache (A. L., N. A.).

Gows∝gi, *(A. L., N. A.), "it smells."*

Catnip
Nepeta cataria (L.)

(1) A hot leaf tea is given to people with colds to make them sweat (M. A.). A tea is given to babies for colds (Minnie Saunooke). A tea for colds (Olbrecht, 1932, L. H.). (2) A poultice of the leaves is made for boils (Betty Owle). (3) A leaf tea is taken as a stimulant, tonic (Betty Owle). (4) A tea is given to depress fevers (Olbrecht, 1932). (5) A leaf tea is drunk to relieve an ailing stomach (Kimsey Squirrel).

Wes daʔu ni gEsti, *(Kimsey Squirrel),*
"cat eats." (Introduced)

Selfheal, Wild Sage
Prunella vulgaris (L.)

(1) Bathe in a root tea when you are bruised (when you turn blue) (Y. J.). "Some of the old timers called this plant 'rattlesnake tail' from the shape of its flower (inflorescence)" (Y. J.). (2) Make a cold water to bathe burns (A. L.). (3) In early spring the plant is used for greens (A. L.). (4) The plant is used to flavor other medicines (H. R.).

Selfheal, Wild Sage
Prunella vulgaris

Ga ni gwi li ski, *(Y. J.), "clotted blood," or "it is bruised,"* I na tu wa ^{dz}i^{+}z$\propto$, *(W. W.),* U^{dz}an ti wa si t$\propto$ná, *(N. C.),* U^{dz}a n$\propto$g$\circ$ta?, *(A. L.).*

Mountain Mint, Mealy Mint
Pycnanthemum spp.

(1) Make a poultice of the leaves for headache (A. L., H. R., Mandy Walkingstick). Eat the leaves for headache (N. A.). (2) Drink a tea for fevers and colds (Mandy Walkingstick, H. R., N. A.). (3) Make a tea of the leaves for heart trouble (M. A.). (4) Bathe with a warm tea for an inflamed penis (A. L.).

Gows$\propto$gi, *(A. L., N. A.),* G^{w}sh$\propto$gi, *(T. L.),* *"it smells."*

Summer Savory
Satureja hortensis (L.)

(1) Sniff of the leaves for headache (W. W., N. A.).

Ga u sha gi, *(W. W., N. A.), "it smells."*

Hairy Skullcap
Scutellaria elliptica Muhl.

see *S. lateriflora* (v).

Skullcap
Scutellaria incana Biehler

(1) The root is one of the ingredients in a kidney medicine (A. L.). (2) A decoction is taken for nerves (M. A.). (3) The root tea is a medicine for female monthly periods (A. L.). The

Skullcap
Scutellaria incana

roots of "it is bruised" and *Helianthus spp.* are boiled into a tea "for young women" (Y. J.).

U?ta nEu da i, *(A. L.), "grand hanging,"*
Ga ni gwi lis ki, *(A. L.), "clotted blood," or "it is bruised."*

Mad Dog Skullcap
Scutellaria lateriflora (L.)

(1) A decoction of the four varieties of *Ga ni gwi lis ki*, *S. lateriflora, S. elliptica, Hypericum spp.,* and *Stylosanthes spp.* is drunk to promote menstruation, and the same decoction is also drunk and used as a wash to counteract the ill effects of eating food prepared by a woman in the menstrual condition, or when such a woman by chance comes into a sick room or house under taboo (Mooney, 1885). (2) A decoction is drunk for diarrhea (Mooney, 1885). (3) The root is used with other herbs in a decoction for breast pains (Mooney, 1885). (4) A decoction of the roots is drunk to get rid of afterbirth. Afterwards, vomiting is induced with a tea of *Polymnia uvedalia* (Olbrecht, 1932).

Gœnil gwœ^d lis ki u tœnɔ, *(Olbrecht, 1932), "clotted blood," or "it is bruised."*

NIGHTSHADE FAMILY *Solanaceae*

Jimsonweed
Datura stramonium (L.)

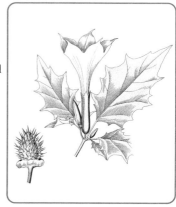

(1) Smoke the dried leaves for asthma (A. L., H. R., Betty Owle). (2) The wilted leaves are heated and applied as a compress to boils (Mandy Walkingstick).

U ni sti lœis ti, *(A. L.). (Introduced)*

Wild Tobacco
Nicotiana rustica (L.)

Tobacco is used by itself or in combination with other plants in a number of the Swimmer Formulas: (1) In Formula 1: "For fever." (2) In Formulas 2 and 82: "For headache." (3) In Formula 3: "For sharp pains." (4) In Formula 42: "For apoplexy." (5) In Formula 47: "For snakebite." (6) In Formula 79: "To dispel witchcraft." Old tobacco is dropped on the fire in the home of a sick person to ward off witches, who prey on the weak (Olbrecht, 1932). (7) In Formula 90: "For boils." The seeds of old tobacco must be sown in November or December because it won't grow if sown later. Regular tobacco is sown in spring. When old tobacco is grown, the leaves must be taken off during a lightning storm, or else one must fast and remove the leaves at noon, not eating until afterward. Old tobacco was not used for smoking or chewing but just used for medicine and to do away with witchcraft, when it is usually mixed with ordinary tobacco (W. W.).

⁺Sɔ·lɑcgɑcyɔli, *(Olbrecht, 1932), "tobacco."*

Ground Cherry
Physalis heterophylla Nees.

(1) The plant has an edible berry (W. W.).

U nEgɑcwis ti ᵈⁱun sti, *(C. S.), "tomato, little,"* U nɑcgu hi·sti u tɑcnɑc, *(W. W.), "they go through, big."*

Horse Nettle
Solanum carolinense (L.)

(1) Pieces of the root are strung and placed about a baby's neck to stop the excess flow of saliva (M. A., A. L.). (2) Cut up the berries and fry them in grease. The grease will then cure dogs of mange (H. R.).

U nu lɑcis tɑc, *(Y. J.),* Kɑcli wɔtiˈno u la nɑchi, *(W. W.),* Go li wodɑc, *(A. L.).*

Nightshade
Solanum nigrum (L.)

(1) If one of the family dies and the others are lonesome and affected by the death, make tea of the leaves and stem of this. Use the tea to vomit in large quantities every fourth day. "To throw up bad saliva" (W. W.). (2) When young, it is made use of as the best relished potherb (Witthoft, 1947b).

SEla̅ u nɑ?gEi̅, *(W. W.), "name black."*

FIGWORT FAMILY *Scrophulariaceae*

Gerardia
Aureolaria flava (L.)

(1) An ingredient in the medicine accompanying Formula 16: "For fainting."

Dɔyi wɔyi, *(Olbrecht, 1932),* Di⁺ɬɑstɛgi is tɛgwɔ, *(Olbrecht, 1932).*

Gerardia
Aureolaria pendicularia (L.)

(1) An ingredient in the medicine accompanying Formula 16: "For fainting."

Di⁺ɬɑstɛgi ˈstɛgwɔ, *(Olbrecht, 1932).*

Downy False-foxglove
Aureolaria virginica (L.)

(1) (1) An ingredient in the medicine accompanying Formula 16: "For fainting." (2) An ingredient in the medicine accompanying Formula 49: "For diarrhea or dysentery." This is used in several medicines (W. W.).

At⁺zaEgwa̅, *(W. W.), "trout, big,"* Di⁺ɬɑstɛgi stɛgwɔ, *(Olbrecht, 1932).*

Common Lousewort
Pedicularis canadensis (L.)

(1) A steep of the roots is rubbed on sores. A prayer is recited (W. W.). (2) "Owl head" is an ingredient in cough medicine (W. W.). (3) A hot root decoction is taken for stomachache (N. S.). (4) An infusion of the roots and leaves is drunk for flux (A. L.).

U gu kɑ u skɑ, *(A. L., N. C.),* U ku ku us ko, *(W. W.), "owl head."*

Common Lousewort
Pedicularis canadensis

Mullein, Mule Tail
Verbascum thapsus (L.)

(1) An ingredient in the medicine accompanying Formula 33: "For pain in various places." (2) Used in the medicine accompanying Formula 56: "For throat trouble caused by insects." (3) A tea of roots is taken for female trouble (Mandy Walkingstick). (4) Rub the leaves under the armpits for prickly rash (H. R.). (5) A syrupy decoction of the roots is taken for coughs (A. L., H. R., Minnie Saunooke). Prepare a decoction of the leaves of Mullien and *Castanea dentata* and mix with brown sugar or honey. Use as a cough syrup (N. A.). Chew the dried leaves for catarrh (Betty Owle). (6) A poultice

made of the dried, shredded leaves in warm water will "take down" the swelling of sores (N. A.). The leaves are used in poultices (Olbrecht, 1932). (7) An ingredient with one or two other herbs in a kidney medicine (Y. J.). A root tea for kidneys (Lloyd Lambert). (8) A tea of the leaves of Mullien and *Y nuᵘniɔya gis ti* (Tradescantia?) is taken for miscarriage (dropped baby's bag) (Y. J.). (9) Bathe in a root infusion for swollen glands (M. A.). (10) Bathe the legs in a root infusion for dropsy (L. H.).

⁺Sɔ·li yus ti, *(N. A.),* U ni kwɔtE·nᵅ, *(Olbrecht, 1932), "tobacco-like, it has down,"* ⁺Sɔ·li yus ti dᶜlɔ·ni, *(Mandy Walkingstick), "tobacco-like, yellow,"* ᵈᶻU skwaɔn ni, *(N. A.), "blanket."*

Common Speedwell
Veronica officinalis (L.)

(1) Apart from the regular medicine which accompanies Formula 75: "For chills," an infusion of "clotted blood" is prescribed for the patient should "he thirst." (2) A

Common Speedwell
Veronica officinalis

decoction including the root of "clotted blood," and the cone of *Pinus pungens,* the stem of *Impatiens capensis,* and the bark of *Ulmas rubra* is given to pregnant women before going to the water each new moon. The bark of *Veronica* will cause the baby to "jump down" quickly (Olbrecht, 1932).

G∝na gw∝^{d}tis ki, *(Olbrecht, 1932),*
G∝ni gwa^{d}tis ki, *(Mooney, Ms.),* "clotted blood," *or* "it is bruised," Ni gɔ^{i}to i taE^{E}i.

TRUMPET CREEPER FAMILY *Bignoniaceae*

Cross Vine
Bignonia capreolata (L.)

(1) A tea made from the leaves cleanses the blood (Witthoft, 1947b).

LOPSEED FAMILY *Phrymaceae*

Lopseed
Phryma leptostachya (L.)

(1) The roots are used in an attraction medicine (love formula). The paired seeds are symbolic (W. W.).

^{dz}is kwa di nɔt∝lu gi, *(W. W.),* "bird, breast sticks out."

PLANTAIN FAMILY *Plantaginaceae*

Plantain
Plantago spp.

(1) An infusion of the leaves of plantain and the stalks of *Juncus tenuis* will strengthen a child when it is learning to crawl and walk. "If they don't walk it's rheumatism" (A. L.). (2) The leaves are used in a poultice for rheumatism (A. L.). (3) A leaf poultice will relieve a headache (A. L.). (4) Apply the wilted leaves to a yellow jacket sting (A. L.). Wilt several leaves and put them on a sore. "It draws up the sore" (L. H.). (5) For snake bite (see *Polygala senega*) (Adair, 1775).

N∝nɔu dEdɔ?ti, *(Y. S.),* ^{dj}u ya ta ɫi ta la wa dÉ, *(W. W.),* "grows around white oak tree."

MADDER FAMILY *Rubiaceae*

Partridge Berry, Squaw Vine
Mitchella repens (L.)

(1) The roots of squaw vine and *Hieracium venosum* are made into a tea for bowel complaint (N. C.). A tea of the whole plant is taken for "summer complaint" (A. L.). (2) A tea of the roots is given to a baby before it "takes the breast" (N. C.). (3) A root tea is taken for monthly period pains (M. A.). (4) If you kill a pheasant and a cat which is going to have kittens eats some of pheasants guts, her kittens won't grow in her and will die after they are born. Make a steep of the leaves and give it to the cat to drink before the kittens are born, and they will grow and live (W. W.).

Tᴐdis ti̡ u ni gis ti, *(W. W.)*, "pheasants eating," Kɬᴐdi sunᴐsti di, *(A. L.)*, Kla dis di u ni gis ti, *(N. C.)*.

Field Madder
Sherardia arvensis (L.)

(1) A red or rose dye is extracted for use with fabrics (Leftwich, 1952, M. A.).
(Introduced)

HONEYSUCKLE FAMILY *Caprifoliaceae*

Honeysuckle
Lonicera spp. (L.)

(1) The vines are used in basketry (Leftwich, 1932: common fact).
(No Cherokee name could be found), e yúh is currently used in Cherokee, NC.- ed.

Elder
Sambucus canadensis (L.)

(1) The berries are used in jellies and other foods (A. L., Y. J.). (2) A decoction made of the roots and the bark is taken for summer complaint (N. A.). A tea of the scraped bark is good for the stomach (H. R.). (3) Elder-berry tea is drunk for rheumatism (M. A.).

Ko?sᴐga, *(A. L.)*, Ko?s ᴐga, *(N. A.)*, "elder."

Maple Leaved Viburnum
Viburnum acerifolium (L.)

(1) This is an ingredient in a tea for smallpox (Y. J.).

Ka ni ga, *(Y. J.).*

Witherod
Viburnum cassinoides (L.)

(1) If the tongue is sore, wash it with a bark infusion of this (T. L.).

Ka ni ga∝, *(Y. J.).*

GOURD FAMILY *Cucurbitaceae*

Gourd
Cucurbita pepo (L.)

(1) An ingredient in a green corn medicine with *Impatiens spp., Zea mays,* and *Andropogon virginicus* (M. S.). In a second green corn medicine (see Appendix) it is an alternate ingredient (W. W.). (2) An infusion made of the mashed seed is drunk to check excessive urination (M. S.).

Ga lu na, *(W. W.),* Ga lu⁺na, *(M. S.), "gourd."*

BLUEBELL FAMILY *Campanulaceae*

Southern Harebell
Campanula divaricata Michx.

(1) A tea make by steeping the root in boiling water is taken for diarrhea (W. W.).

ᵈⁱHi yÉs∝di ki, *(W. W.),* ᵈⁱyÉ ᵈᶻodis ki, *(W. W.).*

Cardinal Flower
Lobelia cardinalis (L.)

(1) An ingredient in the medicine accompanying Formula 33: "For pain in different places." (2) A leaf decoction is drunk to reduce fever (C. S.). (3) A cold tea make of the roots and leaves when sniffed up the nose will stop nosebleed (T. L., N. C.). A cold infusion of the roots of cardinal flower and blue cardinal flower is used for nosebleed (A. L.).

Cardinal Flower
Lobelia cardinalis

Gi ga gÉɑ^{dz}ilɔski, *(Olbrecht, 1932), "blood-like,*
it is a flower," ⁺Sɔli yus ti gi ga gÉA^{dz}ilɔs ki,
(W. W.), "tobacco-like, blood flower,"
⁺Zɑga gɑ^{dj}un tɑnɑ, *(C. S.), "to smell, big,"*
⁺gɔli yus ti a mEu du hi, *(N. C.).*

Indian Tobacco
Lobelia inflata (L.)

(1) The beaten up roots are used in a poultice for body aches (A. L.). Rub the leaves on sores, aches, stiff neck, chapped places, etc. "Don't drink it, it's bitter" (N. C.).

⁺Sɔli yu sti, *(A. L.), "tobacco-like,"* Ski in^{dj}una sa don, *(C. S.), "devil's leg rattle."*

Blue Cardinal Flower
Lobelia siphilitica (L)

(1) A cold infusion of the roots of blue cardinal flower and *L. cardinalis*, is used for nosebleed (A. L.). (2) A poultice of the crushed leaves is used for headache (C. S.). (3) A warm leaf infusion is good for colds (T. L.). (4) A poultice of the roots is applied to a rising (T. L.).

^{dj}ɔli yus ti, *(T. L.),* ^{dz}o li yus ti, *(C. S.),*
"tobacco-like," TsɔlEgwa, *(A. L.).*

Pale Spike Lobelia
Lobelia spicata Lam.

(1) Used in medicine accompanying Formula 40: "For shakes and trembles."

⁺Sɔli yus ti us ti ga gɑt u sEi, *(Olbrecht, 1932), "tobacco-like, small mountain."*

Venus Looking-glass
Legousia speculum-veneris (L.) A. DC.

(1) An ingredient in the medicine accompanying Formula 46: "For indigestion."

U′skw∝y′E lÉ, *(Olbrecht, 1932)*, *"they have it at the top."*

COMPOSITE FAMILY *Asteraceae*

Yarrow
Achillea spp.

(1) Smoke the dried leaves in a pipe for catarrh (C. S.).

S⁽a?so·ᵘni gis tí, *(C. S.)*, *"goose weed."*

Ragweed
Ambrosia spp.

(1) A leaf tea is taken for fever (H. R., M. A.). (2) A leaf infusion is rubbed on for hives (M. A.). (3) When the skin is poisoned, rub on the leaves (A. L.). For infected toes, apply the juice squeezed from wilted leaves (Betty Owle).

U gwa sti lu ᵞᵃd∝, *(W. W.)*.

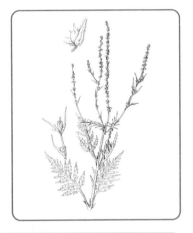

Ragweed
Ambrosia artemisiifolia L. var. elatior (L.) Descourtils

(1) An alternate ingredient in a green corn medicine (see Appendix).

U ni stElEhi stí, *(W. W.)*, *"sticking out."*

Ragweed
Ambrosia trifida (L.)

(1) An alternate ingredient in a green corn medicine (see Appendix) (W. W.).

U gwa⁽ta lu ya d∝, *(W. W.)*.

Pearly Everlasting
Anaphalis spp.

(1) A warm leaf steep is drunk for bad colds (W. W.). A tea of the whole plant is taken for flu (H. R.). Smoke or chew the leaves for bad cold. (A. L., N. A.). (2) For throat infection, blow a warm tea on the tonsils with a tube. A formula precedes the blowing (W. W.). The

Pearly Everlasting
Anaphalis spp.

leaves and stems are smoked for "phthysic," a hanging bronchial cough (M. A.). (3) The dried leaves are a substitute for chewing tobacco (A. L.). (4) To cure a headache or blindness caused by the sun's radiance, make a cold tea of the roots (or in the summer use the leaves and stem). Pour this tea over a hot rock and breath the fumes (Y. J.).

K∝nEsk∝wɔ·di, *(C. S.), "star flower,"*
Ko·stu·d∝, *(W. W.),* K stu d∝, *(Y. J.),*
Koɔstu·da, *(A. L.), "ashes."*

Everlasting
Anaphalis spp.

(1) The dried leaves are smoked for catarrh (C. S.). (2) Drink a warm steep for a bad cold.
K∝nes k∝wɔ·di, *(C. S.), "star flower,"* Ko·stu·d∝·u lÉ, *(W. W.).*

White Plantain
Antennaria plantaginifolia (L.) Hook

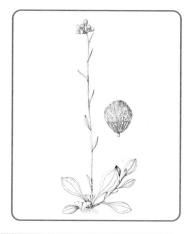

(1) For bowel complaint (when the bowels change color—especially in children) drink a decoction of the entire plant (Y. J.). Boil four "bunches," give to children for summer complaint (A. L.). (3) A tea is taken for excessive discharge in the female monthly period.
Gos du d∝, *(Y. J., T. L.),* Kos tu gu, *(A. L.),*
"evergreen."

Wormwood
Artemisia absinthium (L.)

(1) For children with worms. Gather the seeds in fall, roast and put them in molasses for children (Source unknown).
Gow sh∝di uˡgi waˊ diɬ his do di, *(W. W.), "smell, worm, to kill with."*

Aster, Hardweed
Aster spp. (L.)

(1) A root tea will check diarrhea (Kimsey Squirrel).

A?ta' at∝yu'sti, *(Kimsey Squirrel), "eye like."*

Aster
Aster linariifolius (L.)

(1) Beat up roots in water, sniff up the nose for catarrh (A. L.).

Pale Indian Plantain
Cacalia atriplicifolia (L.)

(1) Held in great repute as a poultice for cuts, bruises, and cancer, to draw out the blood or poisonous matter. The bruised leaf is bound over the spot and frequently removed. The dry powdered leaf was formerly used to sprinkle over food like salt (Mooney, 1885).

Da ye wu, *(Mooney, Ms.), "it sews itself up."*

Plumed Thistle
Cirsium altissimum (L.) Spreng

(1) A warm tea of the roots is taken for overeating (A. L., Mooney, Ms.). (2) The pappus (down) was formerly used to feather blow darts (W. W.). (3) The roots are used in a poultice (Witthoft, 1947b).

^dGi· ^dgi, *(A. L.),* ^dZi ^dZi, *(Mooney, Ms.), "thistle,"* T git gi^{dj}un sti yus ti, *(W. W.), "thistle, little."*

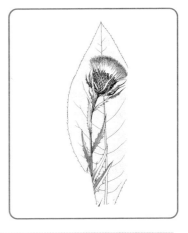

Tickseed
Coreopsis spp. (L.)

(1) Take a root decoction for flux (N. A.). (2) The whole plant is much-used for coloring. It affords a red dye (Witthoft, 1947b).

Tickseed

Coreopsis spp.

Dɔɔlɔni, *"yellow."*

Robin's Plantain
Erigeron pulchellus Michx.

(1) Make a poultice of the leaves for headache (A. L.).
Make a poultice of the roots for "sun pains" (headache)
(M. A.). (2) Drink a cold root tea for colds, or chew the
root and swallow the juice (N. A.).
Tɔɔlɔhi ^{dz}u wa dE sti, *(A. L.), "white oak,
around the,"* ^{dj}u wa dE ti, *(N. A.).*

Boneset, Thoroughwort
Eupatorium perfoliatum (L.)

(1) For colds and sore throat: boil the leaves and roots in water for a while and pour off
part of the water. Allow the plant to steep in the remainder of the water for several hours.
A spoonful of the resulting tea is to be taken every hour or two (M. O.). A tea is made for
fever (W. W., Peter Long). Tea is made for "La Grippe" (Influenza) (M. A., A. L., H. R.). "The
tea caused me to puke...it broke up the colds" (Cam Sneed).
Ga dɔ ^{dz}u (Hi, *(W. W.), "growing on the mountain,"* Ga du·sɔ·Ehi, *(W. W.),
"rejoins," (translation of the English "boneset"?)* Koɬ kɔɬis ki.

Joe-Pye Weed, Queen of the Meadow, Blow Gun Weed
Eupatorium purpureum (L.)

(1) In Formula 62: "For throat disease," blow gun weed is specified as the tube with which

Joe-Pye Weed, Queen of the Meadow, Blow Gun Weed *Eupatorium purpureum*

the medicine must be administered. (2) The root is used in a decoction with another plant for urination (Mooney, 1885). A root tea is taken for kidneys (M. A., L. H.). The roots of queen of the meadow and *Vernonia noveboracensis* are used in a tea for the kidneys (Y. J.). (3) A root decoction is drunk for the female monthly period (A. L., M. S., H. R.). (4) The presence of the plant indicates the nearness of water. (A. L.) (5) After becoming sick from the odor of a corpse, bathe in a root infusion of this (A. L.). (Olbrecht, 1932, writes that the Cherokees in past times kept the body of a deceased person in the home for as much as a week, although he had found no evidence from his informants.) (6) A tea of the roots keeps pregnant women "built up" (M. A.). (7) The stem is used as straw in sucking up water from a low spring (Y. J.).

A maʔditɔʔti, *(W. W.)*, A ma dɔctɔʔti, *(W. W.)*, *"water dipper,"* Ta lu·lú, *(A. L.)*.

Catfoot, Everlasting
Gnaphalium obtusifolium (L.)

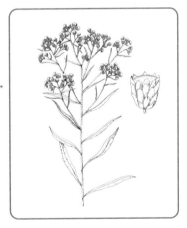

(1) An ingredient in the medicine accompanying Formula 28: "For local pains." (2) An ingredient in the medicine accompanying Formula 62: "For throat disease." (3) A decoction is drunk for colds (Mooney, 1885).

Kɔs tu⁺sɔc, Kas du ta *(Y. J.)*, *"ashes."*

Sneezeweed
Helenium autumnale (L.)

(1) The bruised roots of this and *Vernonia noveboracensis* steeped in warm water, given to women immediately after childbirth, prevents menstruation for two years: then she menstruates once when ready to conceive her next child (W. W.).

Sunflower
Helianthus spp.

(1) Bathe sore feet in an infusion of swamp sunflower (A. L.). (2) The roots of sunflower

Sunflower
Helianthus spp.

and *Scutellaria incana* are boiled into a tea "for young women" (Y. J.).

Dec bni gÉ ga ni gwi lis ki, *(Y. J.),*
"yellow, clotted blood," U na dak?tɔ́, *(A. L.),*
"follows sun."

Large Sunflower
Helianthus spp. (L.)

(1) Chew the whole flower of giant sunflower and the leaves of *Carya spp.* and you spit the color of blood. This might be used as a dye (W. W.).

De lo ni gE·di lɔs ki, *(W. W.).*

Hawkweed
Hieracium venosum (L.)

(1) The roots of hawkweed and *Mitchella repens* are made into a tea for bowel complaint (N. C.).
Tgit gí jun sti yu sti, *(W. W.), "thistle, little, like,"* ^{dj}is tu ga⁺łi, *(C. S.),*
"rabbit's ear," A'wi ga lÉ, *(N. C.).*

Wild Lettuce
Lactuca canadensis (L.)

(1) An alternate ingredient in a green corn medicine (see Appendix) (W. W.). (2) The leaves are eaten in salads (?) (H. R.).

U ni gi so ga hɔ·sti, *(W. W.).*

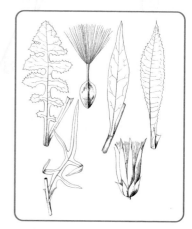

Leafcup
Polymnia uvedalia (L.)

(1) A decoction of the roots of *Scutellaria lateriflora* is drunk to get rid of afterbirth. Afterward, vomiting is induced with a tea of leafcup (W. W., Olbrecht, 1932).

Gɔɔdɔy'ti us ti ga, *(Olbrecht, 1932).*

Gall of the Earth
Prenanthes trifoliolata (Cass.) Fern.

(1) The roots are one of the ingredients used in a stomachache medicine (The other herbs are forgotten.) (N. C.).

Coneflower
Rudbeckia spp. (L.)

(1) Make an ooze of the root in cold water. Drip this ooze from a cloth into an aching ear (N. A.). (2) Bathe sores in a warm infusion (A. L.). (3) The entire plant is used in preparing a brown fabric dye (H. R.).

Nɔda us tiɑ, *(N. C.), "sun, little,"* A? ta, *(A. L.), "eye."*

Orange Coneflower
Rudbeckia fulgida Ait.

Decoction of root drunk for flux and for some private diseases, also used as a wash for snake bites and swelling caused by (mystic) 's ga ya' or worms, also dropped into weak or inflamed eyes. This last is probably from the supposed connection between the eye and the flower resembling an eye (Mooney, 1885).

Aɑwi ak ta, *(W. W., N. C.), "deer eye."*

Coneflower
Rudbeckia laciniata (L.)

(1) Some people grow these in their garden. The plant is a favorite green, eaten when small (T. L., A. L.).

Sɔ+cha ni, *(T. L., A. L.).*

Goldenrod
Solidago spp.

(1) Used in the medicine accompanying Formula 73: "For flux." The roots of two goldenrods are used in a tea for summer complaint (N. C.). (2) A root tea is taken for tuberculosis (H. R.). (3) A root tea is used for neuralgia (M. A.). (4) A tea is made for fevers (Witthoft, 1947b).

Dᴐlᴐni, *(C. S.), "yellow,"* U gu gu shᴐ, *(Olbrecht, 1932), "owl head,"* U nᴇs ti la E gwa, *(N. C.), "they stick on big."*

Marigold
Tagetes spp.

(1) The flowers are used in a yellow fabric dye (Leftwich, 1952).

Ironweed
Vernonia noveboracensis (L.) Michx.

(1) A tea is taken for the female monthly period (A. L.). (2) A root tea will relieve the pains following childbirth (Mandy Walkingstick). (3) The bruised roots of this and *Helenium autumnale* steeped in warm water, given to women immediately after childbirth, prevents menstruation for two years; then she menstruates once when ready to conceive her next child (W. W.). (4) The roots of ironweed and *Eupatorium purpureum* are used in a tea for the kidneys (Y. J.). (5) A root tea is held in the mouth for loose teeth—to harden the gums (A. L.). (6) A tea is made by steeping a large knot of the root in warm water. This tea is drunk for stomach ulcers or hemorrhage from the stomach (M. O.).

Ga ni gwi lis ki, *(N. C., A. L.), "clotted blood" or "it is bruised,"* Kwan dis lok ti, *(W. W.), "purple flower,"* Sᴐna, *(T. L.).*

Cocklebur
Xanthium strumarium Murr.

(1) If a baby is afraid of you and cries when he sees you, get a burr from this plant; touch it against your forehead, and then touch it to the baby's head. The baby will then like you and "hang on to you" (W. W.). (2) If a fish bone or some other object is stuck in the throat,

make a tea of the burrs of this plant and take a large swallow (Y. J.). (3) This and other "stick on" plants are used in a tea to retain the memory in the medicine man initiate (Olbrecht, 1932). (4) A tea of the burrs is taken for cramps (M. A.). "When the top burr is grown, it is time for the frost" (M. A.). (5) Chew the roots for rattlesnake bite (Betty Owle). (6) A root tea is used as an emetic for sick stomach (A. L.).

U nEs ti l∝is ti, *(Y. S.), "they stick tight,"*
U nis ta∝l∝is ti ᵈⁱ∝nEgw∝, *(W. W.),*
"it sticks on, big."

Chapter 4

Cherokee Complaints or Illnesses

1. **Spoiled Saliva (said to be caused by dreaming of snakes):** Dreams of the bite of a snake were considered detrimental to the health of the patient and were treated as seriously as an actual bite because it could cause the spoiling of saliva (Mooney and Olbrechts 1932: 176). Olbrechts described the state of spoiled saliva from dreaming of fish as tasting different, getting thick, and possibly changing color to white or yellow (Olbrechts Ms. 4600). The affliction associated with spoiled saliva was quite serious. A Cherokee who had spoiled saliva was thought to become "despondent, withers away, and dies" (Mooney and Olbrechts 1932: 15).

2. **Thrash:** This is just another name for thrush, a yeast infection of the mouth common in young children.

3. **Milky Urine:** Olbrechts described milky urine, or *unegö tsandiköça* ('if they water out white'), as an infection of the kidneys. But whitish urine, or chyluria, is also associated with tuberculosis and diabetes (Sherman et al. 1987), two conditions that are currently problems among Native Americans (Farrell et al. 1993, Rhoades 1990). Both will be discussed below. Two species of plants with milky latex, *Chamaesyce maculata* and *Euphorbia corollata*, were used in a formula to treat milky urine. Olbrechts tried to symbolically associate these plants with milky discharges (Mooney and Olbrechts 1932: 180), but the majority of the other plants used to treat this condition did not exude milky latex.

4. **Navel Yellowness:** This and the next are probably the same condition.

5. **"when the stomach is yellow":** Bile was considered one of the primary body fluids of the Cherokee, but discussion of it was limited to one ethnomedical condition, *dalâni* ('yellow'). *Dalâni* takes its name from the yellow bile that was observed to be present in the vomit of the patient. Mooney referred to the condition as "old biliousness" and ascribed it to the irregular eating habits of the Cherokee (1891: 365). While Mooney interpreted the Cherokee explanation for *dalâni* as due to the revenge of the terrapin and

the turtle, Olbrechts expands the explanation to include the spirits of vengeful animal spirits. These confound the bile and caused excess to collect in the veins under the navel (Mooney and Olbrechts 1932: 182). In his notes, Olbrechts describes the most common symptoms of *dalâni*, which include a sallowness of the face, black rings around the eyes, dark urine, and a frothy discharge from the bowels (Ms. 4600). In *The Swimmer Manuscript* (1932: 182) he added vomiting of bile and soreness around the navel to these symptoms.

6. "Bad Disease": A condition whose primary symptom was a severe fever. It may have been similar to the intermittent fevers associated with malaria.

7. Ague: Ague is an old name for the flu. (As is "grippe") Also used for any illness with chills, such as malaria.

8. Catarrah: Catarrah is a heavy mucus discharge usually associated with colds.

9. Swelling of leg "caused by biting of spirit insects in the flesh": Olbrechts explained one aspect of this in his notes as this being the spirits of slain insects that were believed to take up residence under a person's skin and cause swellings, blisters, and ulcers (Mooney and Olbrechts 1932: 29). But he also explained it as the condition below in his notes: *aninöskeni yuwot?isö uyot?gisti* – 'if their leg swells and itches.' This was caused by insects seeking revenge for human transgressions. The remedy consisted of making a salve by burning an old shoe to a powder and mixing it with bear's grease.

10. "to take the coat off tongue": *andánkalagísk?* – 'it takes things from around the teeth and tongue' – *Geranium maculatum* L. – wild geranium or *Heuchera americana* L. – alumroot. The name *andánkalagísk?* was one of the few examples of Cherokee names representing utilitarian functions. It originated from the application of these plants to treat conditions like thrush and scurvy and stems from *tstlâskû?* or *tstlâsk?* ('the fire, or light, has gone out'), a form of *ktlâskû* ('the fire is going out'). The name symbolized the alleviation of pain from the mouth and gums.

11. Disordered bile: see Navel Yellowness and "when the stomach is yellow" (these are all different names for the same thing).

12. Black Disease: As far as "black" goes, Olbrechts discussed black *dalâni* ("black yellow"), a condition of deranged bile that causes dark rings around the eyes and the fingers turn black. It was the most serious of the kinds of *dalâni*. It's discussed in The Swimmer Manuscript.

13. **Disordered saliva:** saliva tastes bitter and dry—this is all that has been mentioned about this condition, but it is different from spoiled saliva.

14. **"tired in the chest":** Most likely congestive heart failure.

15. **Bold (Bald) Hives:** A common folk condition in the mountains. Somewhat like a milk rash, but it was considered necessary for the rash to appear externally or the baby would die. Driving the rash inward was considered lethal, so it was an internal condition, but it did need to be brought to the surface. Catnip tea was the most common remedy used to bring the rash to the surface. Another source interpreted bold hives as a type of spirit possession that led to crib death. It is not a skin condition, but the rash is necessary to expel the problem.

—Definitions provided by Dr. David Cozzo,
Professor of Anthropology at the University of Georgia.

Chapter 5

Sacred Formulas of the Cherokee

Some of the most interesting records of Indian lore in all North America are the medicinal formulas of the Cherokee Indians. These records are the only ones of their kind so preserved. The manuscripts, as mentioned in the introduction, are written with the characters invented by Sequoyah in 1821.

The shaman, or medicine man, commonly used his formulas in conjunction with a plant medicine, but some of the formulas call for no medicine. Actually, the formula was regarded as more important than the simple herb or medicine prescribed. The formula was read or recited in a ritual language (Olbrechts, 1932), the meaning of some of the words being sacrificed for exactness of form. Not one word of the formula can be changed, even though the meaning of a phrase might be obscure.

The shaman uttered the formula in a low voice to conceal it even from the person being treated. Only the shamans knew the formulas, and it was common practice for the old timers to trade or sell their formulas. Many, if not all the shamans, recorded their knowledge in notebooks, some of which were collected by Mooney.

Mooney, 1885, writes of Cherokee religion and the importance it played in the formulas:

> "Cherokee religion has... a wonderful completeness about the whole system which is not surpassed even by the ceremonial religions of the East. It is evident from a study of these formulas that the Cherokee Indian was a polytheist and that the spirit world was to him only a shadowy counterpart of this. All his prayers were for the temporal and tangible blessings—for health, for long life, for success in the chase, in fishing, in war and in love, for good crops, for protection and for revenge. He had no great spirit, no happy hunting ground, no heaven, no hell, and consequently death had for him no terrors and he awaited the inevitable end with no anxiety as to the future..."

Olbrecht, 1932, outlines a pattern which the formulas follow, although "...perhaps not one formula is exactly like it, nor does it (the pattern) mention other motives which occur occasionally."

(1) An exclamation invoking the attention of the spirit.
(2) An expression praising the spirit's potency.
(3) The spirit's name, color, and its abode.
(4) The reason for which the spirit's help is invited, a statement of the cause of the inequilibrium.

(5) Some depreciatory remarks leveled at the malignant power.

(6) Some specific reason why the spirit called upon is expected to effect relief in this particular instance.

(7) An emphatic statement that relief has been effected.

(8) A final exclamation.

Throughout the formulas occur numbers and colors which have symbolic significance. The Cherokee symbolism and habitat for each of their colors is listed below (Mooney, 1885). The Cherokee names for the different colors are synonymous with English names; some Cherokee names embrace a range of colors which include several English colors.

Color	Habitat	Symbolism
red	the East	success, triumph
blue-green	the North	defeat, trouble
black	the West	death
white	the South	peace, happiness
brown	above (?)	unascertained, but propitious
yellow-orange	———	about the same as blue

The sacred numbers are listed below (Olbrecht, 1932).

Several of the old numbers have attained a new significance.

4 The fundamental sacred number in Cherokee ritual (from the four compass points?).

7 From the seven Cherokee clans (or as Mose Owle says, the seven days in which God made the earth).

12 The number of scores necessary to win the ballgame (or, according to Mose Owle, the twelve disciples of Jesus).

24 The number of taboo days after the delivery of a baby.

Some of the formulas are quite expressive, especially the formulas which are related to winning the love of a maiden. Below is a sample translation of the formula originally recorded in Sequoyah characters. It is a formula recited during childbirth (Mooney, 1885).

> Listen! you little man, get up now, at once. There comes an old woman.
> The horrible (old thing) is coming, only a little way off.
> Listen! Get your bed and let us run away. Yu!
> Listen! you little woman, get up now, at once. There comes your grandfather.
> The horrible old fellow is coming, only a little way off.
> Listen! Quick! Get your bed and let us run away. Yu!

This formula is designed to frighten the baby into being born. Both a "little man" and a "little woman" are addressed so that the formula will be effective, no matter what the sex of the newborn may be.

The 96 formulas, below, are condensed versions of those discussed more fully in *The Swimmer Manuscript,* Olbrecht, 1932. Given, in this order, are (1) the disease or condition for which the formula is used, (2) the plant, if any, and how they are used, (3) in quotations, a few words giving the general thought of the formula, which is often lengthy. In some cases the formula is very simple, in which the shaman merely names several plants and says to the effect, "This will cure it." The phrases which occur in quotations are not to be taken even as rough translations, they are meant only to convey the general idea of the formula.

Formula 1: For the "Big Chill." A decoction of either wild tobacco, *Nicotiana rustica L.,* or choke cherry, *Prunus virginiana* L., is blown on the patient: "Oh Whirlwind, Thou and I are powerful!"

Formula 2: For headache. Water and the juice of dwarf ginseng, *Panax trifolius* L., (wild tobacco *Nicotiana rustica* L. may be substituted) is blown on the head of the patient: "The wizards have just passed by, they have caused relief."

Formula 3: For when they are sick with "sharp pains." The roots of wild tobacco, *Nicotiana rustica* L., and parsnip, *Pastinaca sativa* L., are chewed: "Oh, Black Raven, put this man back on his feet, only a ghost has caused it!"

Formula 4: For itching. The roots of stickseed, *Lappula* spp., and wild comfrey, *Cynoglossum virginianum* L., are boiled into a tea and applied: "Use these plants, this is all there is to it." The itching here is caused by urinating on a fire, or on some object on which urinating is tabooed.

Formula 5: For when he dreams of snakes. A decoction of the roots of rattlesnake fern, *Botrychium virginianum* L., or Virginia snakeroot, *Aristolochia serpentaria* L., or the bark of tuliptree, *Liriodendron tulipifera* L., is rubbed on to the place where the patient dreamed he was snake bitten. The place is breathed on four times and the patient is given some of the decoction to drink, causing him to vomit: "Oh, Black men, come help him for it was only a ghost snake which bit him."

Formula 6: For urinary diseases (when yellow and white mucus is passed). A bruised root infusion of flowering spurge, *Euphorbia corollata* L., and another unidentified *Euphorbia* is rubbed on and drunk. Fasting is observed until sundown; using two yellow and two red beads on a cloth the shaman prays, "Hear, Oh Red Kingfisher, make the Yellow Chat and the Yellow Frog—who have put the thing under him—release their hold."

Formula 7: For vomiting bile and soreness of the navel region. No herbs are used: "You, Oh Yellow Killdeer and Yellow Fish, take away the Black Man to the night land!"

Formula 8: Similar to Formula 7, no medicine used: "Now then, Red Otter, you will push away the disease spirit with the crown of your head."

Formula 9: For sore eyes. A piece of bark from alder, *Alnus spp.*, is chewed and the juice is blown into the eye of the person suffering from sensitivity to light caused by seeing a rattlesnake: "This will cure you of that which the enemy caused in striking you."

Formula 10: Same disease and cause as Formula 8, no medicine is used: "Oh Miller, Thou Wizard, Thou hast originated on high. Relief has been caused."

Formula 11: As for Formulas 7 and 8, no medicine used: "Ha, Yellow Pigeon and Yellow Goldfinch, take away that which the disease spirit has put under him."

Formula 12: For an incantation disease caused by a maligning conjurer. A handful of branch tips of Virginia pine, *Pinus virginiana,* from seven different trees are boiled in water and then removed and hidden in a dry place. The water is placed in a cup and passed four times in circles above the patient's head, after which he drinks it: "Now then, Yellow Dog, thou wizard, you shall undo the work of the Simulator."

Formula 13: For headache. The medicine is a tea but the original manuscript does not mention what herb is used. "You merely have to say 'Wolf' and blow it on."

Formula 14: For sore navel, no medicine used: "As you have passed by Yellow Pigeon and Yellow Goldfinch, you have taken it with you."

Formula 15: For disordered bile. An infusion of the bark scrapings of Hydrangea, *Hydrangea arborescens* L., and sweet pepperbush, *Clethra acuminata* Michx., is drunk to induce vomiting. The disordered bile is thrown off into the river: "You powerful ones—Yellow Goldfinch, Yellow Pigeon, Long Human Being, White Kingfisher and Red Fish Hawk—have come to push it aside."

Formula 16: For fainting. An infusion of decoction of four species of foxglove, *Aureolaria*, are drunk for four consecutive mornings, with fasting. The three identified species are: fern-leaved foxglove, *A. pedicularia* L., downy yellow foxglove, *A. virginica* L., and smooth yellow foxglove, *A. flava* L.: The fourth species has not been determined. "This is all the different kinds of foxglove."

Formula 17: For children's diarrhea. A decoction of trailing arbutus, *Epigaea repens* L., is drunk: "The sickness is in defecating green and white substance."

Formula 18: For taking a client to the water for various purposes, no medicine used: "The white thread has come down, the soul has been examined..."

Formula 19: For rheumatism. The patient is scratched with a branch of sawbrier, *Smilax glauca* Walt., and eel oil is rubbed on: "This is the treatment when they feel tired."

Formula 20: Medicine for "spoiled saliva" caused by dreaming of snakes. As an emetic, a decoction of great bulrush, *Scirpus validus* Vahl., common rush, *Juncus effusus* L., crown vetch, *Coronilla varia* L., carolina vetch, *Vicia caroliniana* Walt., and poison ivy, *Rhus radicans* L., is drunk for four consecutive days: "Now then, Thunder Boys, remove the snake from under him."

Formula 21: Prescription for aggravated hoarseness. A decoction of the inner bark of five trees: cherry/plum, *Prunus* spp., southern red oak, *Quercus falcata* Michx., or shingle oak, *Q. imbricaria* Michx., flowering dogwood, *Cornus florida* L., apple *Pyrus malus* L., and white willow, *Salix alba* L., was drunk and applied to the throat. The bark was collected from the east side of the tree. No formula was recited.

Formula 22: Medicine for milky urine. A decoction of the inner bark of four trees: *Betula nigra* L., *Quercus stellata*, *Carpinus caroliniana*, *Platanus occidentalis*. "Thou on high has caused the white bone to come down on the body."

Formula 23: Medicine for fever with headache. An infusion of the leaves of chinquapin, *Castanea pumila* (L) Mill., is blown upon the head and shoulders of the patient.

Formula 24: Medicine for sharp pains in the breast. The patient drinks an infusion of bruised Virginia snakeroot, *Aristotochia serpentaria* L., to which a few scrapings of ginseng root, *Panax trifolius* L., are added. "Now then! Ha, now you two have come to listen, you two Red Men, you two are staying in the direction of the Sun Land."

Formula 25: Medicine for rheumatism, languor, and kindred ailments. A warm infusion of the leaves of *Leucothoe catesbaei* Walt., *Kalmia latifolia* L., *Rhododendron maximum* L., *Veratrum viride* Ait., *Porteranthus trifoliatus* L., and Indian physic is rubbed on the ailing spot. "Thou on high has caused the white bones to come down on the body."

Formula 26: For illness with "yellow" (bile?). No medicine is used, only rubbing with warmed hands: "Put the yellow into the lake."

Formula 27: For a fainting cramp with intense pain. As above, rubbing but no medicine: "I have no pain, I have no pain, etc...."

Formula 28: For local pains, twitchings, cramps, etc., caused by dreaming and by revengeful animal spirits. The patient is scratched and infusion of three herbs is rubbed on: saw brier, *Smilax glauca* Walt., wild vetch, *Vicia caroliniana* Walt., and rabbit tobacco, *Gnaphalium obtusifolium* L. "Now then, Red Raven – come take away and eat that which the ghost has put under him."

Formula 29: For when their breast swells. An infusion of four plants is used four times before noon for four days to cause vomiting: horse-balm, *Collinsonia canadensis* L., walking fern, *Camptosorus rhizophyllus* L., wild ginger, *Asarum canadense* L., and sharp-lobed hepatic, *Hepatica acutiloba* D. C. The whole plant is used in every case but the first plant, in which the leaf or root is used. "Ha, two little men from the sunland, you are chasing the important thing back to the great lake."

Formula 30: For fever blisters. A tea of the dried leaves of chinquapin, *Castanea pumila* L., is blown on the sore spot: "Now then, little frost and little frog, take it away."

Formula 31: Same as Formula 25, with a recitation conveying the same idea.

Formula 32: For intestinal worms. A thick, sweetened decoction of Indian pink, *Spigelia marilandica* L., is taken morning and night with massage and blowing: "Now then White Bittern, White Sandpiper, and White Mud Snipe, stick your bills into it and cause relief."

Formula 33: For pain appearing different places. A warm infusion of the roots of great mullein, *Verbascum thapsus* L., and cardinal flower, *Lobelia cardinalis* L., and the bark of speckled alder. *Alnus rugosa* DuRoi, or smooth alder, *A. serrulata* Ait. Willd., is applied to the ailing spot: "Now then, Brown Otter, thou wizard, pull out what is under him."

Formula 34: For vomiting when the stomach is yellow. The patient drinks a warm decoction made of the inner barks of four trees, after which he goes to the water: black gum, *Nyssa sylvatica* Marsh., sweet pepperbush, *Clethra acuminata* Michx., speckled alder, *Alnus rugosa* Spreng, and hazelnut, *Corylus americana* Walt.: "Ha, Weasel, Thou hast pulled out the bile."

Formula 35: For sore eyes. An infusion of the bark of speckled alder, *Alnus rugosa* Spreng, is rubbed and blown into the eye of the patient: "The enemy has hit thee and passed by."

Formula 36: For shifting pains, as in Formula 33. An infusion of the leaves of doghobble, *Leucothoe fontanesiana*: "Now then Brown Eagle, Blue Eagle and White Eagle—carry it off."

Formula 37: For yellow urine. Plants are used with this formula, but are omitted from the Swimmer manuscript: "This will cure you."

Formula 38: For stopped urinary passage. To the infusion of Formula 37 is added seven twigs of sourwood, *Oxydendrum arboreum* L., or black gum, *Nyssa sylvatica* Marsh. This mixture is drunk: "This along with seven twigs will do it."

Formula 39: For dizziness, fainting, or headaches. An infusion of Virginia snake root, *Aristolochia serpentaria* L., warmed by dropping seven live coals into it, is blown on the head, breast and back of the patient: "The wizard from the forest comes with relief in his hand."

Formula 40: For arm shakes and trembles. The affected area is scratched. Over the scratches is blown a cold water steep of spiked lobelia, *Lobelia spicata* Lam. The formula and four applications of the medicine is repeated four times in the morning for four days, if necessary. The medicine is sometimes drunk: "Now then, two Red Men, make the Black Man relinquish his grip."

Formula 41: For chills. A warm infusion of the roots of several ferns: Maidenhair fern, *Adiantum pedatum* L., Christmas fern, *Polystichum acrostichoides* Michx., brittle fern, *Cystopteris fragilis* L., hay-scented fern, *Dennstaedtia punctiloba* Michx., and cinnamon fern, *Osmunda cinnamomea* L., are blown on the patient from the east, north, west, and south, in succession, four times in the morning for four days: "Now, then, Thou Red Man, Blue Man, Black Man and White Man, you will conquer him."

Formula 42: For fits (apoplexy?) A root infusion of dwarf ginseng, *Panax trifolius* L., wild tobacco, *Nicotiana rustica*, sometimes added, heated with four or seven live coals, is blown four times on the patient. "The men have just gone by."

Formula 43: For taking people to water—an involved formula without medicine.

Formula 44: For pains appearing in different places. No medicine is used: "Now then Red Otter, Brown Otter, Blue Otter and Black Otter—take it away."

Formula 45: For pains in the side. No medicine is used: the formula invokes the help of several "men" for relief.

Formula 46: For indigestion from overeating. The patient bathes in the river; and drinks and bathes in an infusion of the bark of honey locust, *Gleditsia triacanthos*

L., and the roots of Venus' looking glass, *Specularia perfoliata* L., and red buckeye, *Aesculus pavia* L.: "This will cure them."

Formula 47: For snakebite. The shaman chews a quid of wild tobacco, *Nicotiana rustica* L., and sucks the snakebite. "Ha, White Fawn and White Lizard, suck it out."

Formula 48: For fever attacks. The patient is washed with an infusion of common flax, *Linum usitatissimum* L.: "Now then, White Fish and Blue Man, take it away."

Formula 49: For diarrhea or dysentery caused by the animal or bird spirits. A decoction of seven plants (one unidentified) is drunk for four days: slippery elm, *Ulmus rubra* Muhl., sycamore, *Platanus occidentalis* L., basswood, *Tilia americana* L., downy yellow foxglove, *Aureolaria virginica* L., northern red oak, *Quercus rubra* L., and white oak, *Q. alba* L.: "Put all these together."

Formula 50: For stomach trouble caused by bad odors. A warm infusion of seven plants is drunk to cause vomiting. Only one plant given in the Swimmer manuscript, rattlesnake master, *Eryngium yuccifolium* L.: "This will cure it."

Formula 51: For menstruating women who dream of giving birth to animals or unnatural beings. A root decoction of plants having roots in the water is drunk: hydrangea, *Hydrangea arborescens* L., sycamore, *Platanus occidentalis* L., and black raspberry, *Rubus occidentalis* L. Salt and hot food taboos, and partial fasting is prescribed: "These will cure her."

Formula 52: For removing worms. A decoction of roots and bark, sweetened with honey is taken morning and night for four days: Indian pink, *Spigelia marilandica* L., small yellow lady's slipper, *Cypripedium calceolus* L. *var parviflorum* Salisb., Fern., and a third unidentified plant. Water, eggs, and greasy foods are tabooed: "Ha, wizard–cure it!"

Formula 53: For water blisters on the body. A warm bark infusion is poured over the afflicted area until the water ceases to run: staghorn sumac, *Rhus typhina* L., or smooth sumac, *R. glabra* L., and winged sumac, *R. copallina* L.: "Now then, Blue Man, take away what the sun has caused."

Formula 54: For abdominal pains caused by the terrapin, or some other animal, spoiling the saliva. The abdomen is rubbed and a plant decoction is drunk to cause vomiting: wild ginger, *Asarum canadense* L., sharp-lobed hepatica, *Hepatica acutiloba* DC.), and trailing arbutus, *Epigaea repens* L.: "Now, White One, make the terrapin relinquish his grip."

Formula 55: For when urination is irregular: A bark decoction using all or part of the following herbs is drunk: strawberry bush, *Calycanthus fertilis* Walt., summer grape, *Vitis aestivalis* Michx., Allegheny blackberry, *Rubus allegheniensis* Porter, hearts'-a-bustin',' *Euonymus americanus* L., fox grape, *Vitis labrusca* L., pepper-vine *Ampelopsis cordata* Michx., and whorled loosestrife, *Lysimachia quadrifolia* L.: If all seven of the herbs are used, a taboo is placed on salt, hot food and sexual intercourse: "This will cure it."

Formula 56: For throat trouble caused by insects (diptheria?). A poultice of the beaten boiled leaves of great mullein, *Verbascum thapsus* L., is applied to the throat; the liquid is blown on: "Now then Brown Frog and Blue Frog chase it away."

Formula 57: For headache. No medicine is used: "Now, Little Man, bring relief!"

Formula 58: For diseases caused by magically introduced objects. The shaman holds a cold bark infusion of speckled alder, *Alnus rugosa* Spreng., in his mouth and sucks the sore spot. The extracted object is spit into a bowl: "Thou, Blue Watersnake, pull out what He has put under him."

Formula 59: For frostbitten feet. No medicine is used: "Oh Red Mountain Lion, cure it."

Formula 60: For prevention or cure of frostbitten feet. The patient puts his feet under broomsedge, *Androgogon virginicus* L., which is believed to warm the feet of wild rabbits: "Ha, rabbit—I have put my feet where it is warm."

Formula 61: For thrash, or sores in mouth. The inner bark of mockernut hickory, *Carya alba* Nutt. is chewed by the shaman who blows it into the mouth of the patient. The family is restricted during the treatment: "Ha, little snow, scatter it!"

Formula 62: For throat disease (diptheria?). A warm decoction of rabbit-tobacco, *Gnaphalium obtusifolium* L., is blown into the throat of the patient with a tube of wide-leaved Joe-Pye weed, *Eupatorium purpurem* L.: "Now then, Fish, scatter them." The ailment is believed to be caused by insects.

Formula 63: For toothache. No medicine is used: "White Squirrel, take away what the ghost has put in."

Formula 64: For breast ache. No medicine is used: "Ha, Red Man, remove the heat."

Formula 65: For navel yellowness. A warm bark infusion of American hornbeam, *Carpinus caroliniana* Walt., is applied four times: "Now then, Yellow Killdeer, fan it away with your wings."

Formula 66: Virtually the same as Formula 44.

Formula 67: For body pains (Rheumatism?). No medicine is used: "Now Black Man and Red Man, remove it beyond the hills."

Formula 69: For shot and arrow wounds. A piece of the inner bark of mockernut hickory, *Carya alba* Nutt., is chewed and blown on the wound: "Now, Brown Dog, stop the bleeding."

Formula 70: For childbirth. A decoction of yellowroot, *Xanthorhiza simplicissima* Marsh., is given to the woman in labor: "Jump down little man (woman) grandma is coming." (A complete translation of this formula is given at the beginning of this section.)

Formula 71: For bowel troubles. A cold infusion of small-flowered agrimony, *Agrimonia parviflora* Ait., is drunk at regular intervals: "This will cure it."

Formula 72: For flux. A decoction of pin cherry, *Prunus pennsylvanica* L., and persimmon, *Diospyros virginiana* L., is drunk: "This will cure it."

Formula 73: For flux. A steep of goldenrod, *Solidago* spp., is drunk: "This will cure it."

Formula 74: For flux. An unidentified fern is used in a steep: In this case there is no recitation.

Formula 75: For chills. An infusion is blown on four times, consisting of cherry or plum, *Prunus spp.* L., black cohosh, *Cimicifuga racemosa* Nutt., white baneberry, *Actaea pachypoda* Ell., and creeping phlox, *Phlox stolonifera* Sims. An infusion of common speedwell, *Veronica officinalis* L., is given to the patient if he thirsts. In this case there is no recitation.

Formula 76: For childbirth. No medicine is used. The formula is similar to that in Formula 70.

Formula 77: For sore abdomen caused by an enemy "changing food." No medicine is used. The shaman entreats to various colored dogs to "remove it."

Formula 78: For bad diarrhea. A root decoction is boiled to thick consistency, watered, and again boiled down, for a total of four times and drunk. The decoction consists of the roots of summer grape, *Vitis aestivalis* Michx., pepper-vine, *Ampelopsis cordata* Michx., flowering dogwood, *Cornus florida* L., black gum *Nyssa sylvatica* Marsh., eastern serviceberry, *Amelanchier canadensis* Medic., and sourwood, *Oxydendrum arboreum* L.: "Oh Great Spirit, thou has given me permission to use it."

Formula 79: For children who cry due to persecution by mountain people. An infusion of wild tobacco, *Nicotiana rustica* L., is blown over the body of the child: "Oh Red Man, break up the ball game which the mountain dwellers play in his stomach."

Formula 80: For itching privates when one has urinated on a fire. The roots of_ Virginia snakeroot, *Aristolochia serpentaria* L., or tuliptree, *Liriodendron tulipifera* L., is chewed and the juice is blown into the urethra by a grass stalk or cane tube. An infusion of the same plants is drunk. In this case there is no recitation.

Formula 81: For when he urinates yellow. A root decoction of calamus, *Acorus calamus* L., spring iris, *Iris verna* L., virgin's bower, *Clematis virginana* L., and Dutchman's pipe, *Aristolochia macrophylla* Hill., is drunk two or four times: "Cure him, Oh Sun and Little Men!"

Formula 82: For headache. The root of wild tobacco, *Nicotiana rustica* L., or dwarf ginseng, *Panax trifolius* L., is chewed and the juice is applied to the head and neck: "The Red and Purple men have scattered it." (Compare with Formula 2.)

Formula 83: For going to the water and examining with the beads. No medicine is used; a prayer is said to the river.

Formula 84: For sore places (rheumatism). A stamper is made of the wood of persimmon, *Diospyros virginiana* L., which is pressed to the sore place: "The Little Wizards have chased it away." A fee of a knife is charged.

Formula 85: For yellowness of the navel. No medicine is used. The patient is rubbed with warm hands while the shaman entreats to various birds.

Formula 86: For indigestion and biliousness. A root decoction is poured over hot rocks in the sweat house. The decoction, which is also drunk as an emetic, consists of speckled alder, *Alnus serrulata* Willd., persimmon, *Diospyros virginiana* L., cherry or plum, *Prunus* spp., sycamore, *Plantanus occidentalis* L., tuliptree, *Liriodendron tulipifera* L., and cucumber tree, *Magnolia acuminata* L.. In this case there is no recitation.

Formula 87: For frostbitten feet. No medicine is used, the treatment consists of recitation and sucking: "I am a wolf," etc.

Formula 88: For boils caused by caterpillars. No medicine is used, the shaman only touches the patient with his heated thumb. The recitation is untranslatable, being a series of magic words.

Formula 89: For headaches. No medicine, the treatment consists of rubbing and blowing: "Relief is caused."

Formula 90: For boils. The juice of wild tobacco, *Nicotiana rustica* L., is rubbed on the boil: "Relief is caused."

Formula 91: For pains caused by the heat spirit (rheumatism). No medicine is used; the shaman massages the patient: "Oh Blue Man, cure him."

Formula 92: For bad dreams. No medicine is used to prevent the ill effects of the dreams, the patient is "taken to the water" by the shaman and the formula, an entreaty to various animals, is recited.

Formula 93: For "going to the water" to help oneself. The person says a prayer to the "Long Man"; takes no medicine.

Formula 94: Medicine for when they urinate white. A warm infusion of *Euphorbia corollata* L., flowering spurge, *Euphorbia hypericifolia* L., spurge, *Echium vulgare* L., viper's bugloss, blueweed, blue devil is drunk. There is no recitation.

Formula 95: Medicine for when their urine is milky. A warm infusion of black gum, *Nyssa sylvatica* Wang., and smooth alder, *Alnus rugosa* (Du Roi) Spreng., is drunk all day the first day, then until noon the second day, and until 10 a.m. the third day, and until just before breakfast the fourth day. Hot food, salt and sexual intercourse are forbidden.

Formula 96: Medicine for when a tooth comes out. Throw the tooth on the roof of the house, while asking the beaver to give a new one. "Beaver, put a tooth in my jaw!"

Chapter 6

The Green Corn Ceremony

The Green Corn Ceremony is all but forgotten among the Cherokees today, but less than a century ago it was an integral part of Cherokee culture and religion. A statement by Witthoft, 1949, sheds some light on the origin of the rite.

> "For some centuries prior to the appearance of Europeans on the North American continent, the aboriginal peoples of the Eastern woodlands and of the Eastern plains shared an economic culture complex that depended largely upon agriculture and chiefly upon one plant, *Zea mays*."

The extreme dependance on corn soon became manifest in cultural myths. Two versions of the story SElu, the corn mother (SElu is also the Cherokee word for corn) were told to Witthoft, 1947a. The versions differ only in details: each relates the history of SElu, her hunter husband, Kanati, and their two sons.

The first son of SElu was of natural birth but the second son was born of magic, and he was wild and hard to control. One day when the father was on a hunting trip the sons plotted to spy on SElu, to discover where she procured the corn and beans with which she fed them. Following her into a storehouse and concealing themselves, they watched her beat upon herself as the corn fell from beneath her skirts. She then rubbed her armpits and produced beans. The son of unnatural birth became enraged (according to one version, because he thought her a witch, and a second version, because he thought she was feeding excrement to her family) and killed SElu. Subsequent to this slaying the first corn plant grew.

An earlier account of the myth (Mooney, 1883) states that before she was murdered, SElu pleaded with her boys to enact a ritual with her body. She instructed them to keep an all-night vigil on the place where her body would spill so that they would be provided with corn the next morning. Later, when the corn seed was distributed to all people, it was found that the corn would not grow unless an all-night ceremony was held. Thus was initiated the sacred Green Corn Ceremony.

The myths continue to tell how wild animals escaped from Kanati's store den and are now found throughout the woods, and that Kanati and his two sons became the thunder people.

Charles Hicks, 1818, a principal chief of the Cherokees, recorded in a letter appearing in a newspaper story the earliest known account of a Green Corn Ceremony. The people would gather in different towns at night about large fires. The conjurer in charge took some of the grains from seven ears of corn and fed them to the fire. (An offering to the thunder boys?) All the people attending would drink a tea of wild horehound, *Lycopus virginicus L.*, ... Later in the season, when the corn was getting hard, the green corn dance was held. The dance lasted four days, near the season when the national council was in session.

Exactly what the belief common to all or most of the Cherokee may have been and what purpose of the dance and ceremony might have been, it is certain that the original significance has been altered. Frank G. Speck (Witthoft, 1949) described a modern green corn feast which he said was not held at any fixed time of the year. Speck observed that the feast seemed to have lost all connection with the cycles of the agricultural year. He concluded that it was performed for curative purpose and spiritual benefit at whatever time in the summer it may have been needed by persons desiring spiritual help.

Will West Long described such a festival (Witthoft, 1947a) which he stated was held the night before the first corn was to be eaten. This ceremony was probably observed by Will during his lifetime but the writer doubts if anything like it can be found or even described today. A few of the conservatives like Will West Long clung to such tradition, and remained unchanged by Christianity.

According to Will's account, the festival began with all participants taking medicine causing them to vomit. This was followed by "going to the water" and bathing for purification. A series of animal and social dances followed which lasted all night.

In the morning the conjurers, who were also the dance leaders, examined each person with the beads and the cloth to see whether they would live until the next year's green corn festival. Two beads were used: one red (or white) and one black. The beads were laid on a cloth furnished by the examinee and kept as a token by the conjurer. After a formula was recited, the beads were watched. If a black bead moved the person was sure to die unless a special ceremony was enacted. The person was safe for another year if the red bead moved. Witthoft, 1947a adds that a second portion of the obsolescent Green Corn Ceremony became separated into a second observance. This is the green corn medicine which is prepared in the individual households of the more conservative Cherokees. It is administered to all members of the family as a prerequisite to the eating of the green corn. Mandy Walkingstick told the writer that her grandfather gave a nasty-tasting tea to his family once a year before eating the corn. The tea was drunk for breakfast of the day corn was to be eaten. The ingredients which Mandy's grandfather used are the same as those used by Mollie Sequoyah's family. The reason given for the use of the medicine is "to prevent colic," which would plague anyone eating the green corn without previously taking the medicine. It is especially necessary for children. The tea is made of the leaves of the following plants:

Cucurbita spp., Gourd   Ga lu na, *(W. W.)*, Ga lu⁺na, *(M. S.)*, *"gourd."*

Andropogon virginicus L., Beard grass   Se lú kwayɔc, *(W. W.)*.

Impatiens pallida Nutt., Jewelweed,   Wa lElú unig lE gis ti,

(N. C.), Wa lElú una^dz i la gis ti, *(N. C.)*,

Zea mays, Volunteer corn, Se lu kwo yá, *(W. W.)*.

A more complicated medicine was prescribed by Will West Long, to overcome the generative power which corn imparts to intestinal worms. It was (perhaps is) believed that corn silk is transformed into intestinal worms if swallowed.

The plants used in Will West Long's Green Corn Medicine are as follows:

Andropogon spp., Beard grass; KᴐnEskᴐc wᴐ·di, *(Olbrecht, 1932),* SE lu Kwayᴐc , *(W. W.).* "resembling corn."

Yucca filamentosa L., Adam's needle; Se lu kwo ya, *(W. W.).*

Amaranthus spinosus L., Spring amaranth; To lEti yu sti, *(W. W.), "stick on you, like."*

Zea mays L., Volunteer corn; Se lu *(N. C., A. L.), "corn,"* Se lu gᴐcwatᴐc, *(M. S.), "corn wild,"* ᴐc wo sa·ul si yEn hi, *(W. W.) "it came up by itself."*

Lactuca canadensis L., Wild lettuce; U ni gi so ga hᴐc· sti, *(W. W.).*

Impatiens capensis Meerb., Orange touch-me-not, Jewelweed; WaᴐlElu unig lE gis ti, *(N. C.),* Wa lElu una^{dz}i la gis ti, *(N. C.),* "hummingbirds taking sap out of the flower."

Cucurbita spp., Gourd; Ga lu na, *(W. W.),* Ga lu⁺na, *(M. S.), "gourd."*

Amaranthus retroflexus L., Green amaranth; Wats′ka, *(W. W.).*

Ambrosia trifida L., Ragweed; U gwa′ta lu ya dᴐc, *(W. W.).*

Cynoglossum virginianum L., Beggar's lice, Wild comfrey, U nis ti l iEsti gwᴐ, *(Olbrecht, 1932), "they make them stick to it, the little one,"* U nis ti lu is ti, *(Mooney, Ms.), "something that sticks to the clothes."*

Ambrosia artemesiifolia L. var. elatior L. Descourtil, Ragweed; U ni stElEhi sti, *(W. W.), "sticking out."*

The use of the first three plants is obligatory, and any one of the others may be used as the fourth ingredient, more being added if available. Will West Long explains that these weeds are used because they are rampant weeds in the corn fields.

Other green corn medicines are listed in the text.

The following quotation from Coon, 1950, is included in his discussion of rites intensification. It is thought applicable at this point.

> "From time to time crises arise which disturb everyone equally because they come from outside the group concerned; ...Here the holy man...shows his versatility, for he conducts mass ceremonies to allay these dangers by magical means, and actually succeeds in uniting the people into a common effort with zeal replacing fear and confusion. In a country where the seasons differ greatly and the annual cycle involves changes of human activity, such ceremonies become annual."

Chapter 7

The Ballgame

This ballgame today plays but a small part in the culture of the Cherokee Indian. It was not too long ago, however, when the ballgame played a highly important role in the Cherokee social life. More than a contest of endurance and skill, the ballgame embodied myths, celebrations, ceremonies, dances, and gambling. The entire community took a more or less active part in the ballgame. The following account is borrowed in part from Mooney, 1890, and from the descriptions of Mandy Walkingstick and Minnie Saunooke, who have witnessed the ceremonies.

The season of the ballgame was from mid-summer to cold weather. The game provided an activity in the slack season after the crops were in (or harvested) when there was nothing to do. The season ended with the coming of cold weather because of the abbreviated costumes in which the natives played.

The weeks prior to the contest were spent in sober preparation. Mooney, 1890, writes:

"As speed and suppleness of limb and a considerable degree of muscular strength are prime requisites in the game, the players are always selected from among the most athletic young men, and to be known as an expert player was a distinction hardly less coveted than the fame as a warrior. To bring the game to its highest perfection, the best players voluntarily subjected themselves to a regular course of training and conjuring; so that in time they come to be regarded as professionals who might be counted on to take part in every contest..."

The night before the game each side held a secret dance. The location of the ceremony was concealed from the rival team lest a spy steal away a trophy ensuring his team of success. The location selected, however, was invariably close to a stream. Shortly after darkness fell over the mountains the dance began.

Three fires were kept burning on the ceremonial ground. The spectators, gathering near the fires, came prepared for an all-night stay. Near one fire danced seven women, representing the seven clans of the Cherokees. The women danced in a line, moving toward and then away from a frame on which several ballplayers' sticks hung. When the female leader of the group was not dancing she was required to stand on rocks.

Around a second fire danced a circle of men, the ballplayers. As the athletes moved about the fire they made feints and motions as though the game were in progress and a ballstick were in each hand. A man with a rattle danced about the ballplayers in a still larger circle.

The third fire was that of the medicine man's. All fires, this latter one in particular, were closely guarded against "enemies." The theft of a glowing ember meant certain defeat. Providing a steady beat for the dancing was the drummer. The drummer was carefully selected, for his was an important position. While pounding on his skin drums he sang of the game on the morrow, of the fine things to be won by the men of his party, of the joy with which they will be received by their friends on their return from the field, and of the disappointment of their rivals. These declarations were said in a loud voice with the rhythm to which the Cherokee language so wonderfully lends itself.

"Ani ge ya   tsu na li i   osda   u ni ge lv hes di   u ga da ta lo sv i"
(Our girl friends will be proud of us when we win the game) (Mandy Walkingstick).

To the drummer's remarks the dancers would shout in unison, "Ha! Ha!"

The woman leader would also sing her declarations:

"Da gi ga ti le gi   a gi go wa ti no   Ayv   hi a sga i hes di"
(When your challenger sees you he will tremble) (Mandy Walkingstick).

All the players would shout their approval at such a boast.

A dancer named *Da la la* (woodpecker) would, during the dance, rush to the edge of the darkness, raise his hands to his mouth and utter four yelps, suggesting the cry of the woodpecker, the last of which was prolonged. He would then rush back to the group and shout:

"A ne tso   u ga tse li hi" (The game is ours!) (Nancy Walkingstick).

The players danced all night and were subjected to strict taboos and observances. The men were not to eat or sit down all night. They could not touch a woman, or vice versa, nor could they touch a child. Frequently they were taken to the water by the medicine man. The many taboos and beliefs are reflected in an old Cherokee myth: (Ibid)

"Many years ago the animals challenged the birds to a game of ball. The bear, the deer and the terrapin—strong by strength, swiftness and armor—rejected two small players who sought to be on the team. The two tiny beasts turned to the eagle and the hawk. The birds won the contest with the help of their new allies."

Not too long ago the Cherokee ballplayers still invoked the aid of the bat and the flying squirrel: a small piece of the bat wing was tied to their ball sticks to impart the quality of evasiveness. Additional taboos were observed 24 days before the game and involved eating restrictions:

(1) Rabbit - he is easily scared

(2) Frog - his bones are easily broken
(3) Fish (hog sucker) - his movements are sluggish
(4) Atunká salad, *Chenopodium album,* - their stems are easily broken
(5) Salt and hot food.

At daybreak the players were marched to the site of the ballgame which was several miles away. The march lasted until noon, as every player was taken separately to the water on the way.

On arriving at the playing field, the ballplayers were scratched and medicine was applied. In a more recent times the instrument used for scratching was a comb provided with seven sharply pointed teeth of turkey bone. When this was not available it was substituted by broken glass, a brier stem or a rattlesnake tooth.

A specific pattern of scratching was prescribed. Starting with either arm, the seven-pronged instrument was brought down four times from the shoulder to the elbow. The other arm was treated similarly. Taking the first arm again, the motions were repeated four times, from the elbow to the wrist. This was done also to the other arm. This procedure was repeated on the legs, beginning with one leg from thigh to knee, and so on. The instrument was then used to scratch an "X" on the back and the chest. In each case another scratch on the back and the chest joined the tops of the "X." Altogether there were almost 300 scratches on the ballplayer. These were but skin wounds, but the blood ran freely. The medicines were applied to the scratches.

A variety of herbs were used by the various medicine men in connection with the ball play. A sample list includes the following, all of which were used as tea steeps and applied in one way or another:

Tephrosia virginiana L. Pers., the toughness of the root was transferred to the muscles.

Juncus tenuis Willd., the sturdy character of its stems kept the player from falling down.

Carya spp., made the limbs supple.

The players were taken once more to the water, a prayer was said with the black and red beads, and the game began. In more recent times uniforms consisting of a pair of shorts were donned.

The ballgame, in one form or another, existed in Indian groups all over North America. In the Cherokee version of the game the number of players is variable, from nine to 12 usually, but an equal number of players are on each side. When the teams have met on the field, excess players are eliminated until the teams match. During the game no substitutions are allowed. If a player on one team should, for one reason or another, have to leave the game, a player on the other team also retires.

The field occupies a flat piece of ground with two uprights at either end, resembling the goal posts of football. A goal is scored when the ball passes through the goal, regardless of whether it is thrown or carried through. The first team to tally twelve goals wins the contest. The number 12, as mentioned elsewhere, has a magical significance from this source.

The ball, a rough, leather-covered sphere, is about one inch in diameter. The ball must not be picked up with the hands. Each player carries in each hand a stick which is equipped at the end with a pocket. At the beginning of the game the ball is tossed into the air and the players endeavor to catch it with their sticks. After the ball is thus caught, the player may hold it in his hand or mouth or he may throw it towards the goal or to another player. James Mooney (Ibid) records the following vivid description of a ball game:

"An old man now advances with the ball, and standing at one end of the lines delivers a final address to the players. He concludes with a loud Taldu gwu!" (now for the 12!) "and throws the ball into the air." Instantly 20 pairs of ball sticks clatter together in the air, as their owners spring to catch the ball in its descent. In the scramble it usually happens that the ball falls to the ground, where it is picked up by the more active than the rest. Frequently, however, a man will succeed in catching it between his ball sticks as it falls, and disengaging himself from the rest, starts to run with it to the goal; but before he has gone a dozen yards they are upon him, and the whole crowd goes down together, rolling and scrambling over each other in the dust, straining and tugging for possession of the ball, until one of the players manages to extricate himself from the struggling heap and starts off with the ball. At once the others spring to their feet and, throwing away their ball sticks, rush to intercept him or prevent his capture, their black hair streaming out behind and their naked bodies glistening in the sun as they run...It is a very exciting game, as well as a very rough one."

In closing this account a quotation from *A Reader in General Anthropology* (Coon, 1950) is thought fitting:

"Among human beings one other kind of competitive effort is universal, besides warfare: that of playing games...Games serve a number of purposes...they take up slack time...They give people a routine to follow when they have come together for a ceremony...They give rival institutions a chance to work off steam, and furnish the routine, the context, of many ceremonial occasions."

Chapter 8

Basketry

The following account of Cherokee basketry is taken from Speck, 1920, and Leftwich, 1952. To this day many Cherokees, residing in more remote sections of the reservation, depend on basket making and other crafts for a portion of their income. Leftwich describes the past and present market outlets for Cherokee crafts:

> "For a long time there were only small shops selling handicrafts on the reservation. It was a familiar scene to see Indians traveling along the road from farm to farm and town to town with their backs piled with an assortment of colorful baskets. After the Great Smoky Mountains became a national park and good roads were built over the surrounding mountains, making it possible for visitors to reach Cherokee easily, it was no longer necessary for the Cherokee to leave the reservation to sell his wares."

Today, the Cherokee use a variety of locally growing materials for basketry. Prior to 1924, only three materials were used in the actual construction of baskets: oak and cane were used for splints, and hickory bark for finishing the rims. Add to these honeysuckle stems, a basket material adopted from the Western Cherokee in 1924, and the most-used materials are listed. More modern Cherokees use other materials due to the influence of white craftsman and the teaching in the Cherokee School. Such recently exploited materials include willow twigs, pine needles, spruce bark, hemlock bark, etc.

White oak, *Quercus alba* L., is the most-used for box splints in Cherokee basketry. The trees selected are straight saplings not over eight or 10 inches in diameter. Most basket makers use only sapwood, but sometimes the heartwood is dyed and used. The splints are stripped from sections of green log from which they part quite readily. The strips are smoothed and gauged with a knife prior to the soaking and dying which precedes the actual basket making.

River cane, *Arundinaria tecta*, Walt., Muhl., and cane *A. gigantea*, Walt., Chapm., were originally secured along the flats of the Tuckasegee River, where small stands have been seen by the author. Speck states, "the restricted locations which they now occupy are somewhat too elevated and cool for the cane to flourish in the immediate neighborhood."

Cane stalks need only peeling and soaking prior to basket making. Some 54 canes, each divided into four pieces, are required for a medium-size wastebasket.

Of incidental interest in respect to the shortage of cane on the Cherokee Indian

Reservation is the treaty signed by the Cherokees and the people of Barbourville, Kentucky in the summer of 1950. The treaty agrees to give, free of charge, all the cane which the Cherokees wish to have.

The preamble of the treaty (requoted from Leftwich, 1952) reads:

"We, the people of the Cherokee Nation, and the people of Kentucky, in friendly council here assembled, do make this solemn compact, to last until such time as the sun shall no longer shine, the birds no longer sing, and green things no longer grow on earth."

The bark of hickory is made into a withe to bind down the rim hoops. An Indian used this material to repair the broken lid of a wicker handbag owned by the writer's wife. The use of hickory bark in the former manner constitutes an ear mark of Cherokee basketry, distinguishing it from the basketry of all other southeastern tribes.

Speck lists six types of baskets which were at one time commonly made:

(1) Pack baskets – made of oak splints, had deep bodies and flaring necks. Their capacity was about one gallon. A strap worn over the head was used to carry the basket.
(2) Fish baskets – made of oak splints, measured from 10 - 16 inches in height. Their bottle neck was preferred by Indian anglers.
(3) Rib baskets – made of oak splints, were made by fastening two oak hoops in a perpendicular position, one hoop being the handle and keel, the other being the basket rim. The spaces in between were filled with the under one, over one technique. Cherokee women used this type for a market basket.
(4) Covered baskets – were made of oak splints. This oblong, peck-size basket was used in the household. Its design was the over two, under two weave.
(5) Low-sided rectangular baskets – were made of either oak or cane splints. Of no particular weave, this basket was used for a variety of household needs: food receptacles, for sifting, straining, etc.
6) Double weave basket – was a cane basket. The splints were laid down diagonally at the bottom and in weaving they are continued obliquely up the sides. The cane strips are sometimes used double, the smooth surface both on the outside and the inside.

Originally only two artificial colors were employed in dyeing Cherokee baskets. These were a black from black walnut, *Juglans nigra* L., and a red from bloodroot, *Sanguinaria canadensis* L., These are now supplemented by a number of other natural stains, listed in the text, and various commercial dyes. Dying takes from one to eight hours depending on the material being dyed, the strength of the dye and intensity of the color desired. Cane is quite hard and requires a longer time for processing.

Summarizing the place of basketry in Cherokee culture and making a comparison with the basketry of other Indian groups, Speck, 1920, writes:

> The only industrial art which has endured long enough among the Cherokee people to afford a prespective is that of basketry. Comparing the basketry of the various southern tribes, the perfection of technique seems indeed to improve as we pass from the Cherokee westward in the Gulf culture area. On the whole the Cherokee as a tribe seems to be about the poorest of the cane basket makers. The fact that oak splint basketry is quite common among the Cherokee seems to lend additional weight to the assumption that the cane actually has been for some time in a state of decline among them.

Xanthium strumarium, 112
Xanthorhiza simplicissima, 33, 37, 44,
50, 61
Xyridaceae, 26
Xyris caroliniana, 26, 31

Y

Yarrow, 105
Yellow Dock, 45
Yellow Fringed Orchis, 33
Yellow Poplar, 51, 52
Yellow Touch-me-not, 75
Yellow Twayblade, 33
Yellow-eyed Grass, 26
Yellow-eyed Grass Family, 26
Yucca filamentosa, 31

Z

Zea mays, 23, 24, 75, 103
Zizia aurea, 84